DECLUTTER
AND
Thrive

OVERCOMING 6 COMMON DISORGANIZATION TYPES TO REVEAL
your best you

DECLUTTER AND Thrive

OVERCOMING 6 COMMON DISORGANIZATION TYPES TO REVEAL *your best you*

DENISE ALLAN
& VLASTA HILLGER

Niche Pressworks
Indianapolis

DECLUTTER AND THRIVE
Overcoming Six Common Disorganization Types to Reveal Your Best You
ISBN-13: 978-1-946533-25-8

Copyright © 2018 by Denise Allan and Vlasta Hillger

All rights reserved. No part of this book may be used or reproduced in any manner whatsoever without prior written consent of the author, except as provided by the United States of America copyright law.

For permission to reprint portions of this content or bulk purchases, contact Denise Allan at denise@simplifyexperts.com
http://SimplifyExperts.com

Published by Niche Pressworks, Indianapolis, IN
http://NichePressworks.com

Printed in the United States of America

DEDICATION

To each and every one of our clients with love and appreciation.

Thank you.

CONTENTS

Dedication v

Foreword ix

Preface xiii

Introduction 1

Six Behavior Types of Disorganized People 5

The Power Shopper 13

The Paper Magnet 31

The Inspired Hobbyist 47

The Caregiver 63

The Easily Distracted 77

The Overburdened Employee 97

The Clutter Clearing System 113

Conclusion 131

Resources 133

Thank You 135

About the Authors 137

FOREWORD

The first time I met Denise Allan was in Stamford, Connecticut—not exactly a hotbed of disorganization or a magnet for professional organizers, and yet there we both were.

We were on retreat, and despite being in business for over 20 years, I was also the new kid in town. Now, if you've ever been the new kid, you know how uncomfortable it can be to take those first few steps into a crowded room where everyone else seems to have known each other for years.

I heard bursts of laughter and conversation ripple around me. My eyes scanned the room, moving from table to table, looking for an open seat. My face flushed and my temples started to pound. I eagerly hoped that something would happen soon to break the mood in the room or give me something to do so I wouldn't feel so awkward and alone. I found an empty seat near the front of the room and sat down.

Just then, one of the retreat staff rang a bell and everyone began to quiet down. The morning session would begin with us going around the room, one by one, and introducing ourselves. I sighed a little, feeling relieved that the first exercise of the day was something I was good at. I've got my elevator speech down, and I speak for a living, so I wasn't too concerned about what I'd say when it was my turn.

Our facilitator, Fabienne Fredrickson, chose a table across the room to start. Denise Allan was the second person to speak.

Denise stood up in a bold and confident way and said her name. She told us that she was from Seattle and had a thriving professional organizing business there. I froze.

I never thought there might be other organizers attending this event. How could I speak frankly about my business with a competitor in the room listening? This was going to suck.

When it was my turn to speak, I said, "I'm Andrew Mellen and I'm 'The Most Organized Man in America.'" The room broke into laughter and Denise looked over at me and made eye contact. We smiled at each other, but I still didn't know how this was going to work. I would soon find out.

90 minutes later we got our first break and before I could bolt out of the room, Denise walked up to me. Strode is more accurate—she has a direct, no-nonsense way of doing most everything, including walking.

She introduced herself and we started talking. Denise's warmth and dry sense of humor instantly put me at ease, and any resistance or concern about her being "the competition" quickly fell away.

For all the work I do helping other people change, I sometimes struggle with my own adaptability. It's funny how we as humans are wired to meet change—sometimes we embrace the adventure and the unknown and other times we fight as hard as we can to resist anything shifting, even when we want or need something to change. It's further proof that logic can only get you so far—just because we want or need something, there may still be internal resistance that defies simple suggestions and common sense.

They say that fear and faith can't exist in the same space. That morning, I let go of fear and stepped into faith. I could tell that Denise was serious about her work and is a kind and thoughtful person. I reminded myself that there is plenty of work to go around. America's love affair with stuff is not going away.

And it was fun exploring our shared passion for helping people simplify their lives. Once Denise and I started talking shop, I knew not only was there nothing to fear, but more importantly, I had just made a new friend and colleague.

That was a few years ago, and since then, we've had the chance to really get to know each other, sharing the ups and downs that come with helping people change their lives. We spent 3 months supporting each other as accountability partners, a technique Denise shares in this insightful book. We spoke every morning at 6:30 a.m. Pacific Time, detailing what the day ahead held for each of us and what we needed support with to ensure that when we spoke the next day we would be more likely to report that we had accomplished the tasks we outlined the morning before.

Given the amount of clutter we surround ourselves with here in the U.S., it's not surprising that there are more self-storage facilities in America than there are McDonald's restaurants. I wonder how many of those storage units are filled by people with Chronic Disorganization?

People who are chronically disorganized struggle with things on multiple levels, sorting through and clearing clutter being just the most obvious one.

If you or someone you love suffers from Chronic Disorganization, this may sound familiar. Ordinary tasks take on a degree of intensity that seems exaggerated; complex tasks can feel impossible. Underlying it all is often a pervasive, almost constant sense of failure and hopelessness.

Until now.

Remember, just because we know something should change, doesn't always mean we have the ability to make that change easily. And if you're scared, a potent blend of faith and concrete actions may be just the solution you need.

That's why the book that you're holding in your hand is so useful.

This is a guidebook that shows you how to identify your disorganization type. And once you do that, you're much closer to addressing patterns of behavior that you didn't even recognize, or may have previously confused or disappointed you.

With this clarity, you may finally be able to break the cycle of frustration and despair that is a common fate for someone who is Chronically Disorganized.

So whether you can't stop shopping, love paper, skip from hobby to hobby, are caring for others, or struggle with time management or disorganization at work—you're going to see yourself in the stories in the book.

More importantly, you'll gain insight into strategies Denise has successfully used with her clients to change weeks, years, and sometimes decades of entrenched behavior for the better.

Denise is one of a handful of professional organizers who is an accredited Master Trainer in Chronic Disorganization, and she knows her "stuff." Whatever your particular challenge, you'll find plenty of smart and practical tips and tools to help you organize your stuff from an expert in our field.

Andrew Mellen

Life Hacker + Professional Organizer

New York City

PREFACE

For years, I've been told—Denise, you *need* to write a book—but I prioritized growing my company, Simplify Experts, to meet the needs of my clients. That was until my team member, Vlasta Hillger, suggested we write a book together, and I discovered we could publish a book, focus on clients, and help even more people realize the possibility of living an organized life. Sounds like a win-win-win!

I'm a lifelong organizer. On my kindergarten report card, my teacher commented that "Denise should stop organizing her tablemates' art supplies and work on her own projects." Even at age six, I was organizing other people's things! Since then, I've raised a family and worked in the non-profit sector fundraising.

Eventually, I took a leap of faith. I followed my passion and started my own organizing business. Every day, I get the privilege of helping individuals and families reduce and manage the chaos, stress, and burden of modern life. It doesn't get better than that!

Vlasta also caught the organizing bug early in life, but it wasn't until she had children that she realized just how much being organized helped her cope with the demands of motherhood. Her son was diagnosed with ADHD and anxiety, and she found that creating a simple, clutter-free environment helped him focus and remain calm.

Every day I hear from clients how overwhelmed they feel. How the state of their homes—the clutter and disorganization—impacts their ability to live their lives. They tell me:

"I've tried to stay organized, but with the kids and my job, it's impossible."

"At the end of the day, I just shove it all in the closet and close the door—just to have some peace."

"There is stuff everywhere. We have not had friends over in I don't know how long."

"I am concerned about my job. I'm ill prepared and barely holding it together."

I have worked with thousands of clients in the Seattle area. They come from all walks of life—single individuals, professionals of varying ages, families just starting out with young children, families with busy tweens and teens, empty-nesters, and those looking to downsize.

I love each of these groups because they all have unique organizing challenges. The reason they seek help from a professional organizer is because they are all coping with the challenges that modern life presents.

Over and over, I've observed that despite best efforts, more and more people are struggling to keep up with the day-to-day demands of life. Technological advances have caused the workday to become interwoven with personal time, to the point that people are never truly "off." The incoming tide of communication, data, news, marketing messages, opinions, and expectations of productivity/efficiency is overwhelming.

Even those who would typically call themselves organized are finding themselves stretched. Their lives might appear Instagram lovely, Pinterest-worthy, enviable even. But on the inside, many Americans are feeling stressed and anxious. Part of this stress and anxiety is the result of disorganization. When a big life event comes along—when people lose or change jobs, move to a new city, have children, face an illness in the family, or the death of a loved one—their ability to cope with the demands of day-to-day life becomes truly compromised.

Sound familiar? Well, I have good news! Overcoming disorganization can become a reality for anyone! The key is to build awareness of what's behind disorganization and create shifts in habits that will bring you closer to living your ideal life. You can do this! And you don't have to do it all on your own. Sometimes the most effective strategy is to get support from a professional organizer.

Getting organized and staying organized is similar to getting in shape and staying in shape. Everyone knows it takes dedication and hard work to get in shape. While we may do our best to follow a training plan, oftentimes, we'll get better results working with a personal trainer who pushes us a little harder and supports us with their experience and knowledge. I will help you examine where you are and where you want to be in order to help you overcome disorganization.

Together, Vlasta and I hope to help you create an organized life that will allow you not just to keep up with the day-to-day demands of life, but to move beyond those demands and live your best life! Take the first step—declutter and thrive!

INTRODUCTION

If you spend an hour a day looking for lost items, you are giving up one week of your year. You deserve so much better than that. This book provides the tools and strategies you need to get on the right path. It is written for anyone who wants to be more organized, but anyone who is chronically disorganized will benefit the most. If you constantly find yourself trying but never succeeding at getting organized, then you *know* you need help. Don't wait any longer!

Your home should support your life, not hinder it. The very definition of home is a place that contributes to your sense of well-being, security, comfort, and rejuvenation. What would it be like to live an organized life?

Imagine feeling the relief of coming home and being welcomed by tranquility. In the entryway, you have a place for your shoes, coat, purse, and keys. There is a place to set down the mail.

In the kitchen, tidy drawers and clear counter space beckon you to begin making or serving a delicious dinner. You look forward to sharing a meal with your family.

You walk into your bedroom and are greeted by a restful, calm atmosphere where you can curl up with your favorite book. It whispers rejuvenation. Your bedroom closet has ample space for your clothes, shoes, and accessories.

You easily find what you need for whatever task is at hand. You can plan and execute tasks, and at the end of the day, you feel accomplished. You feel ready for whatever awaits you tomorrow.

In the morning, you leave home in peace, ready to tackle the day. At work, you are productive, make progress, complete tasks, and plan for what is ahead. You look forward to being home. Your home is a comfortable haven, refueling your energy reserves even when life becomes extra challenging or throws you a curveball.

We want to help you grasp this vision. It is not out of reach for you. You deserve it, and you need it to live the best version of yourself. This book will help you alleviate feelings of being overwhelmed, anxious, and stressed due to disorganization. You *can* live an organized life!

How This Book Works

After years of working with clients, we've identified six of the most common disorganization behavior types. Each chapter focuses on a specific type of disorganization behavior. While we can all learn from these different categories, some sections are more likely to resonate with you than others. Consequently, we've arranged the book so that you can skip around, reading the chapters in any order.

The six different behavior types we address include:

- The Power Shopper – anyone who struggles with shopping and the volume of stuff in their homes.
- The Paper Magnet – anyone who struggles with paper clutter.
- The Inspired Hobbyist – anyone who crafts and struggles with the sheer volume of hobby materials.
- The Caregiver – anyone who feels overwhelmed as they oversee the care of others.
- The Easily Distracted – anyone who struggles with focus, productivity, and/or time management demands.
- The Overburdened Employee – anyone who struggles with disorganization at work.

Every chapter in the book is organized the same way. We begin with stories describing two real-life clients we've worked with and the organizational issues they have faced. We've taken care to alter these stories to protect the identity of our clients.

The next part of the chapter digs into the details of that particular disorganized behavior type. We provide proven strategies to help deal with these organizational challenges—strategies we have successfully used with hundreds of clients. Whenever appropriate, we give additional real-life examples relating to the organizing strategies.

Finally, we return to our client scenarios and share what happened after we worked with these clients. We explain how we approached their challenges and what strategies we used. Each chapter ends with a summary of the topics discussed and additional space for notes.

Then, we pull it all together in chapter 8 where we provide detailed information on how to approach a reorganization using our proven Clutter Clearing System.

It is a proven five-step methodology that should be used when organizing at home or in the workplace, whether alone or with a professional organizer. This methodology includes:

- How to identify a vision for the space to be organized.
- How to sort your items, including tricky objects such as heirlooms.
- How to assign a home for your stuff.
- Strategies for containing items and labeling.
- Tools for maintaining an organized home or workplace.

Remember the vision of a home that supports and enhances your life? This book gives you the best strategies and advice that we use with our clients. You can achieve this goal and it's not something you need to do alone.

Chapter 1

SIX BEHAVIOR TYPES OF DISORGANIZED PEOPLE

When a potential client calls, we first discuss problem areas the client hopes to address. What they tell me usually fits a theme I've heard before. For some people, what leads them to reach out for help is the overwhelming volume of stuff and clutter in their homes. Others call because they are truly struggling with what to do about the piles of paper everywhere. Some are struggling with time management and productivity at home or at work, while others are no longer able to enjoy their hobbies because their homes are so cluttered and full. And some clients would say that they struggle with all of the above!

Have you tried to get organized in the past, but found that your efforts just didn't make the lasting progress you'd hoped for? Has this trend lasted for many years? Have you felt that disorganization has been impacting your life in negative ways? If you have, you are most definitely not alone.

Professional organizers use the expression chronic disorganization, a term defined by the Institute for Challenging Disorganization to describe individuals whose quality of life is suffering because of clutter and disorder.

What are your organizational challenges? The quiz below helps us to categorize the different types of disorganization. Are you curious about which behavior type fits you best?

The Quiz

Read the following list of 30 questions and circle the numbers you think apply to you. Then, go to the key and find all the numbers you circled. This should give you an idea which of the six behavior types best describes you.

1. Do you have many brand new items in your closets with the tags still attached?
2. Have you ever been sent to a collections agency due to unpaid bills?
3. Do you find it hard to prioritize what's most important to do?
4. Are you behind on your own health appointments, but schedule everyone else's appointments?
5. Has anyone ever described your hobby inventory as excessive?
6. Is your marriage suffering due to the requirements of caregiving?
7. Do you find shopping or browsing online stores a source of entertainment?
8. Do you have hundreds of pieces of unopened mail?
9. At work, have you had to recreate a document because you could not find it?
10. Does your employer owe you money because you haven't submitted expenses?
11. Are your task/to-do lists all over the place?
12. Do you have all the supplies for multiple projects that you have not started?
13. Are you frequently too tired to tidy up?
14. Are you finding yourself staying longer and longer at work because you struggle to finish projects?

15 Is an amazing sale price on an item too good of a deal to pass up? Even if it is an item you don't need?

16 Do you browse social media instead of jumping into the thing you need to do?

17 Is your creative area/working space so full of items that you are unable to create in there?

18 Are your work deadlines a huge source of stress and anxiety?

19 Are you behind in paying your taxes?

20 Do you often purchase gifts or decor for others "just because"?

21 Do you worry almost every day that there is something you are forgetting?

22 Do you know the names of several employees at your favorite department store?

23 Do loved ones' or a child's appointments or schedules require multiple hours of driving each week?

24 Do you struggle with time? Does time get away from you?

25 Do your boss and coworkers regularly tease you about your messy desk/office, and it's no longer funny?

26 Do you have hobby/sports gear that has not been used in years?

27 Is it hard to recall the last time you felt rested and not stressed?

28 Do you subscribe to magazines about your interests but never find time to read them?

29 Do you have many purchases still in bags or shipping boxes because you don't have the room to put them away?

30 Do you have piles of papers in multiple rooms or multiple paper stacks on the floor?

The Key

Compare your circled question numbers from the quiz to the key below. The category where you have the most circled answers signifies your primary disorganization type.

Are you a Power Shopper?
You circled question number: 1, 7, 15, 20, 22, 29

> Shopping gives you a rush. Whether it's the mall, online, or big-box stores, you love shopping. You love having the latest fashion, home decor, and the newest electronics. It's hard to resist a new product. Your home is full of stuff, and you don't know where to put it. If it's on sale, it's yours! If you find something beautiful, you will always buy it. If it promises to make your life better, then of course you need it!

Are you a Paper Magnet?
You circled question number: 2, 8, 10, 19, 28, 30

> Your paper piles have reached a tipping point—literally. They are falling over. You don't open mail. You lose important documents and receipts. You are late paying bills. You fear being audited; hence, you retain all possible documentation. Your business paperwork is commingling with personal paperwork. Your file cabinets are full, so you can't use them. You print out hundreds of pages. Whenever you research something, you collect ALL the available pamphlets to get ideas.

Are you an Inspired Hobbyist?
You circled question number: 5, 12, 15, 17, 26, 28

> Your hobby projects have come to a standstill. You have so many wonderful ideas, but you just don't have enough time. Your hobbies are more than just play; your product is your legacy. You've been told you are quite skilled. You've begun many projects but finished few. You have materials for your hobby which have gone out of style. You get inspiration and buy materials frequently.

Are you a Caregiver?
You circled question number: 3, 4, 6, 13, 23, 27

> Everything else must take a backseat to caregiving. You are the primary caregiver to many. You've been able to stay organized in the past, but now you use all your time and energy caring for others. It's impossible to keep up. Family relationships are strained. You experience constant pressure. You have no time for yourself.

Are you Easily Distracted?
You circled question number: 3, 7, 11, 16, 21, 24

> The demands on your time are endless. Your to-do list never gets done. You are only able to put out the fires. Constant distractions break your focus! When a task is hard, and you can't bear it, you procrastinate, choosing to do something fun instead. You just can't stick to the priorities. You commonly think to yourself, where has all the time gone?

Are you an Overburdened Employee?
You circled question number: 9, 14, 18, 24, 25, 30

> Your disorganization at work thwarts your career success. You are working hard, but your performance reviews are worse each year. Your nerves are shot. It's hard to focus with coworkers dropping by. The emails keep coming in, and it's hard to stay on task. You often work late to catch up or meet deadlines. It has become hard to disengage from work. Being disorganized at work is taking a toll on your whole life. You experience constant pressure. You are disorganized both at work and at home.

Now that you've determined the type of organizational challenges you face, it's time to evaluate what needs to be done. For the purposes of this book, we first want you to think about your specific disorganization habits. Read the chapter (or chapters) that most apply to you, so you understand your habits and how these can be changed. Then, it's time to think more specifically about how to get it done.

Sadly, many clients feel shame about their inability to get organized. Often they feel that they need to get organized on their own—that it's their burden to bear.

We've worked with some clients who sleep in a guest room or on the couch because their own beds are not accessible. Others have been unable to pay their taxes because the paperwork is buried in piles. Some have stopped using their dining room because the table has been a repository for various delivery boxes. One client hired me to help organize his bedroom—but the only way to enter that bedroom was to climb in through the window. The doorway was impassable. These are examples of the negative impact of disorganization—the consequences challenge you every day.

Organizational skills do not come naturally to everyone. To have shame about being disorganized is like being ashamed for not being good at math or science. If it's not your talent, it's okay! As my good friend, professional organizer and speaker Andrew Mellen said, "disorganization is your problem, but it's not your fault."

Disorganization is not something you need to overcome alone. In fact, we recommend working together with someone who will cheer you on and stick with you throughout the process. In chapter 8, we talk about finding an effective partner to ensure organizing success. But let's start by looking at each behavior type and the specific, proven strategies that help deal with these organizational challenges. Don't wait any longer! Let's get started!

Chapter 2

THE POWER SHOPPER

Shopping gives you a rush. Whether it's the mall, online, or big-box stores, you love shopping. You love having the latest fashion, home decor, and the newest electronics. It's hard to resist a new product. Your home is full of stuff and you don't know where to put it. If it's on sale, it's yours! If you find something beautiful, you will always buy it. If it promises to make your life better, then of course you need it!

Client Scenarios

Laura's New Condo

Since her divorce two years ago, Laura moved from a 5,000 square-foot home in an affluent suburb to a two-bedroom condominium. Laura reserves one of the bedrooms for her daughter Emily, who is away at college. Laura is sensitive to the fact that she can no longer afford the lifestyle she had during her married life, but the adjustment has been challenging.

Laura loves fashion. Being well dressed is a must. For Laura, clothes shopping is almost a daily routine. She loves where she lives, central to shopping and restaurants. Her only complaint about the condo is that it lacks adequate storage space.

In her previous home, Laura had a spacious walk-in closet. Now, Laura stores her clothes, handbags, and shoes in the closets of both bedrooms, and she has two extra freestanding clothes racks. She becomes frustrated when she must rummage through two closets to find what she needs.

For the past two years, Laura has been traveling extensively, but now she is beginning a job search. Recently, she learned of an exciting new job opportunity. When shopping for a new outfit for her interview, she wasn't sure what she wanted, so she bought several outfits to choose from, spending over $2,800. When she brought her purchases home, she was frustrated and disheartened because she was unable to find space for her new purchases in her closet. She had to keep the clothes in the store bags on the floor of her daughter's room.

When Laura first called us, she wanted to find out how to best store her wardrobe. Later, she nervously admitted that she had to get a job and reign in her travel and shopping because over the past two years she had spent most of her divorce settlement. She noted how disappointed she was not to have been hired for the job she interviewed for.

On the surface, the issue bothering Laura was a lack of storage space in her condo, but several deeper issues were in play. She was facing financial insecurity because of her lifestyle habits.

Michelle's New Carpet

Tom and Michelle both work full-time at a large tech company. They have a 13-year-old son, Zachary, and a 10-year-old daughter, Amanda.

After years of wear-and-tear, they need to replace the carpet in their house. The carpet installers need all the floor space in the house to be easily accessible. Michelle reached out for help because the clutter and volume of their possessions was making it difficult to prepare for this project, and each family member was contributing to the situation.

Tom's office is his man cave—incredibly full and cluttered. It's where he keeps all his electronics projects, sci-fi movies, CDs, and books. He's not excited about having to pack up and move the items to a storage room. He also loves building LEGO™ sets with Zachary. In fact, in their basement playroom, more than 50 large sets built by Tom are on display on shelves. Large bins of extra LEGO™ pieces are stored on the floor of the playroom.

The children's closets don't have any more space for their toys. Zachary has stuffed animals and even more LEGO™ sets displayed in his room. Amanda has a large American Girl® doll collection, including several clothing and accessory bins for her dolls. Michelle has no idea how to begin packing up the kids' rooms.

Michelle, herself, has a spacious walk-in closet, but over the years, it has become packed. The floor of the closet is constantly littered with shoe boxes and laundry. She is ready to let go of some of her old clothes, and she hopes to find a better solution for her shoes.

Michelle was paralyzed, with no idea how to proceed to get their home ready for the carpet installation. By the time she hired us, she had already postponed the project twice.

A house is just a pile of stuff with a cover on it.

– GEORGE CARLIN

Are We a Nation of Power Shoppers?

In short, yes. In our experience as professional organizers, we've seen countless homes where the volume of "stuff" gets in the way of the family's ability to function. Their possessions have become a source of stress and anxiety, rather than pleasure or purpose.

Of course, our possessions matter to us immensely; they have both emotional and functional value. Some things give us a sense of comfort when we come home at night. Others connect us to our past. And some of the things we own just make living easier. We all need "stuff." We don't need so much stuff that it overwhelms us.

In our culture, a benchmark for success is having the most—and best—stuff. We work hard, play hard, and we reward ourselves. We live in a time of unprecedented variety and abundance of consumer products. We see our peers enjoying a certain lifestyle and strive for the same. There is nothing inherently wrong with any of this. You are certainly not a horrible person for wanting stuff. We all do!

But, our stuff becomes a problem when the volume tips the balance to the point where our homes can no longer support us. It's remarkably easy to slide down the slippery slope of a little too much into overabundance. This is exactly what's happening to many people, including our clients Laura, Michelle, and Tom.

So, how do we slip into overabundance? And what can we do to avoid it? We need a strong sense of awareness of the forces at play—the various influences which lead us to overshop. With that knowledge, we can make intentional decisions and protect our homes from becoming overwhelmed by clutter.

Each of the following sections targets a specific power-shopping category and will help you build an awareness of the habits that are adding stress to your life.

Constant Messages to Buy

It's really no wonder that many of us have so much stuff in our homes. Our economy relies on consumer spending. We are bombarded with advertisements and marketing campaigns. These began in the 1950s with catchy ad jingles and permeated pop culture in the 1980s. Today, targeted ads follow us around from page to page on the internet.

Given all the messages to buy, it's hard to avoid becoming a bit like Pavlov's dog, salivating at the sight of our favorite store's catalog. Advertisers have mastered the psychology of marketing, and they know exactly what to do to make us buy. And so, we buy—on Black Friday, Cyber Monday, and every other day of the year.

Sometimes we shop because it is just so easy and convenient. Our entire generation grew up hanging out at the mall. We learned to shop like it was a sport. Today, we can meet friends, go to the movies, get dinner, and shop—all in the same place. And, the internet and shopping apps have given us unlimited, 24/7 access to shopping. It's way too easy to acquire things. Eventually, we run out of places to put all the things we've bought.

By the time a package arrives on the doorstep, it's possible we've already forgotten what we bought. Recently, on Amazon Prime Day, one client placed 52 orders. Fifty-two! Many of these purchases went unopened for months, creating clutter in her home.

For some, ironically, the mall has become a place to escape from their purchases. A client admits that she doesn't like to be at home because it's too cluttered and chaotic. She likes to go to the mall where the hallways are clean and brightly lit, and the shops give her a hopeful feeling.

How do we protect ourselves from these overwhelming signals coming at us at every turn? We need to keep our eyes on the prize—the value of having an organized life.

An organized environment brings calm and ease to our lives. An orderly home is a haven—a place away from life's stressors. Being organized makes every part of the day calmer, less taxing. It means being able to begin the day with full energy reserves. These are goals worth striving for.

When making purchases, we should be mindful of the messages we hear and ask ourselves these questions:

- Do I like this item because I've seen ads for it on social media or in my web browser?
- Would I even be thinking about buying this item if I wasn't at the mall or online right now?

- Do I already have a similar item which would perform the same duty?
- If I don't buy it, will I miss not having it?

Overabundance and Our Collection

As the adage goes, new shoes can cure the blues. And they can… sometimes. We may come home giddy with our new purchase, whether it's a new pair of shoes, a kitchen gadget, or a collectible.

Whatever the item, we are adding to an existing "collection." Over time, our purchases reach a point where the volume of our collection hovers between healthy abundance and a cluttered, stress-inducing mess. Maybe we can't fit all the shoes in the closet (and sometimes we may even forget about some of the shoes we own!). Perhaps we can no longer put outfits together because our clothes are jammed in so tightly that it's impossible to see what we actually have.

Do you have an overabundant collection controlling your space? When our collection reaches this tipping point, it becomes apparent that something must change. We know we don't like how the clutter makes us feel. To avoid repeatedly slipping into overabundance, when deciding on whether or not to purchase a new item, it's important to ask ourselves some difficult questions:

- Do I have space for this item?
- Is this item better than something I already have? Am I willing to donate or discard that item in my collection to make space for this new one?
- Does this new item fill a purpose in my collection?
- Or, as Marie Kondo, an organizing colleague asks us, does this item spark joy? We would like to add a follow-up to that—does this item have a practical use?

If the answer to any of these questions is no—if you don't have the space, if you already own something better, or if this item doesn't fill a purpose in your collection—then you can make an informed decision when choosing whether or not to buy.

Similarly, we once worked with a client who collects model train sets. Although, they hired us to help organize their children's toys, we found that almost every closet and storage space was filled with various trains and train tracks. The overabundance of model train sets left no space for other items. After applying some of the above questions, he conceded that perhaps he did have more tracks than he could ever use, and he let some of the collection go, creating storage space for other items.

> **I define power by having the confidence to make your own decisions and not be swayed by other people.**
>
> –Adele

FOMO and Decision Fatigue

As shoppers, we are all occasionally affected by FOMO (fear of missing out) and by "decision fatigue." Together, FOMO and decision fatigue alter how we behave when we shop, without us even realizing it.

We may experience FOMO when we find an item on clearance, see a sign reading "only three left in stock," or learn that a sale is ending. Even hearing about a new product from a friend can trigger an impulse to buy. When we have a conversation with a coworker about an item they've bought, we may find ourselves thinking "I want that," which can be a result of FOMO.

We all have a fixed capacity for good decision-making in any single day. When we've used this up, the result is often a phenomenon called decision fatigue. The basic idea is that our brains process an astounding amount of information every hour of the day.

As the day wears on, our brains become tired, and therefore, we may make different choices in the evening than we might have made in the morning. So, when we shop online late at night, we may be more susceptible to the influence of ads and sales, causing us to buy more than we might otherwise.

Just like we are advised not to shop for groceries on an empty stomach, we need to be mindful when we shop when tired or late at night. We need to pause before clicking on the "confirm purchase" button and ask ourselves:

- Am I only buying this because it's easy, and I am tired?
- Am I buying this because I saw that my friends have it?
- Am I buying this because I want the lifestyle it represents?
- Am I buying this because I feel I deserve to have it too?

Acquiring for Our Future

We acquire "stuff" to satisfy our perceived vision of the future. When we go through any big, life-stage transitions (e.g., getting married, having a baby), we visualize our bright future and select products to go along with that vision. We strive to live up to an image of success, and there are plenty of products out there that seem to be required.

Wedding registries are an example of acquiring for our future. We register and shop for what we think we might need. We may not even have a house yet, but we've already begun filling it up. In anticipation of motherhood, we begin nesting to prepare the home to be perfect for baby—we organize, decorate, and buy supplies. We acquire volumes of clothes, baby gear, supplies, and toys, filling up the nursery. Or, maybe we think we might want to get a puppy in the future, so we begin buying supplies and toys today.

Whatever the event, when making purchases for the future we should ask ourselves:

- Am I buying based on a perceived or an actual need?
- Am I shopping for items related to something that might or might not happen?
- Am I shopping for something I hope will happen, but may not actually happen?

If you find yourself consistently buying for an event that is not a certainty, then it may be wise to think twice before completing the purchase.

Tech—The New Bling

Tech products are the newest luxury item. Shoppers wait in lines for hours to purchase the latest gadgets. Every day, new products hit the market. New smart phone? We want it! New gaming consoles? The kids love them. New sound system? Yes, please! But here's the rub—technology evolves quickly, and devices soon become obsolete.

Updating tech isn't a one-and-done task. When we replace a device, we often need to retrieve or delete data from the one it's replacing. Because of the threat of identity theft, we need to dispose of or recycle devices safely. Disposing of outdated electronics is not always easy. As a result, we may have closets full of old computers, cell phones, gaming consoles, tablets, laptops, monitors, and cameras—as well as all their associated cables, memory cards, chargers, and batteries.

We tend to store old devices indefinitely, figuring we will dispose of them later (along with all the giant cardboard packaging). But, when these old items stay in garages and closets, taking up valuable storage space, they contribute to the anxiety-causing clutter in our homes.

When shopping for new tech devices, we should consider the following:

- Is this new device a replacement or an addition to my home?
- Do I have the space to store it?
- Am I ready and committed to fully migrate data to my new device?
- Is it time to donate or recycle my old devices to make space for the new?

It's best to resist that new purchase until you're ready to let some of your old devices go.

The Allure of Free Stuff

Buy one, get one free. Redeem this free offer. Receive a free gift with purchase. Who doesn't love free? Who doesn't love a great deal? We certainly do. A good deal or a great find feels like a small victory. But these so-called freebies add to the volume of possessions in our lives—many of which are never used at all, filling our closets and piling up on the floor.

One client we worked with frequently shopped for beauty products. As a result, she often received free product samples. She accumulated so many samples that the volume completely overwhelmed not only her closets, but her entire bedroom as well. Those "free" samples weren't really free. They cost her the use of her bedroom. After many hours working with her to sort and organize, she ended up donating five large bins of new beauty products and samples to a local shelter.

When shopping, we should think realistically about needs versus wants:

- Is this "great deal" the thing that is missing from my collection?
- How much of this product is enough?
- Am I only buying this because it is such a good deal—I don't actually need it?
- Will it take me a lifetime to use up what I already have?

Thrive in an Organized Life

The messages coming at us from all directions to buy, buy, buy are very strong. It is unrealistic to expect that we can somehow block them all out. That is not the goal. But, by asking ourselves the questions in this chapter, we can begin to keep the volume of stuff in our lives at a manageable level.

Imagine this:

- A neat, tidy clothes closet with enough space to easily slide hangers, retrieve clothes, and put together favorite outfits.
- A roomy bedroom that is a calm, pleasant oasis.
- Shoes sorted by type, all in your view, stored in a shoe rack. Handbags organized in their own designated space.
- Children's toys organized in labeled bins and easy to put away at the end of the day.

- A designated space to hang coats and backpacks for every member of the family.
- Drawers and cupboards with enough space to easily move items around and see what's inside—organized and labeled so all family members can return items to their homes.
- A kitchen with clear, open spaces.
- A garage with space for the car as well as bins that hold gear, holiday decorations, etc.

Is your home a living space or a storage space? The best way to protect our home from overabundance is to become aware of our shopping habits and be mindful of the forces influencing us. We need to repeatedly ask ourselves questions about our purchases. This should slow down the tide of items coming in to our homes.

What should you do about the clutter already accumulated in your home? We need to continually engage in decluttering. If you feel ready to reduce the existing clutter in your home and get a fresh start, skip to chapter 8—the Clutter Clearing System. It spells out the exact process to follow. But remember, existing clutter need not be tackled alone. We are here to help!

The Inventory Card

For individuals with overabundant collections, after decluttering using the Clutter Clearing System, we may create an inventory card they can keep with them when they shop. If the client is trying to become more aware of their clothes shopping habits, for example, we will document how many items they own in each clothing category. The client can refer to the card when shopping and make more informed decisions about their purchases.

Post Decluttering Sample Inventory Card

Tops

15 t-shirts (5 white), (2 red), (3 grey), (5 miscellaneous)

10 blouses

12 tank tops

3 heavy sweaters

6 lightweight sweaters

14 workout tops (7 short sleeved), (7 tank tops)

Bottoms

10 pairs of jeans (2 black), (6 blue), (2 white), (1 red), (1 grey)

8 pairs of yoga pants

7 pairs of pants (non-jean)

5 skirts

Dresses

3 semi-formal dresses

6 summer dresses

2 formal gowns

Shoes

4 pairs of athletic shoes

3 pairs of sandals

8 pairs of boots (4 black), (2 brown), (2 grey)

4 pairs of wedges

6 pairs of flats

> **Coats**
>
> 2 black wool coats
>
> 3 lightweight coats
>
> 1 jean jacket
>
> 2 windbreakers
>
> 2 down vests
>
> 2 ski/waterproof winter jackets

A good guideline to keep in mind is having twice the tops as you have bottoms. The above example shows a wardrobe of 60 tops and 30 bottoms. Keep in mind there is no right amount of clothing. Your wardrobe should meet your lifestyle needs and fit in the available storage in your home.

Compulsive Shopping

A common theme in the topics discussed above is overshopping. But sometimes there is a more serious problem called compulsive buying, which goes far beyond a typical power shopper's purchases. It is a serious addiction with individuals to shop constantly to fill a void or need.

The technical name for this affliction is Compulsive Buying Disorder (CBD) or Oniomania. Common characteristics are:

- Having an overwhelming and irresistible need to buy.
- Being constantly preoccupied with shopping.
- Continuing to shop despite negative consequences (financial, relationship, or professional hardships).

Compulsive buying is often a coping mechanism for something deeper:

- **Anxiety** – The only time the individual feels they can manage something is when shopping; completing a purchase delivers a tiny sense of control in life.
- **Depression** – Sometimes overshopping is a reaction to a life trauma. For some, it can be a relief from a stressful life situation (such as being a caregiver to many or feeling overburdened at work). For others, compulsive shopping can be a response to scarcity in childhood. Or, it can be a mechanism for coping with a profound loss.
- **Low self-esteem** – The individual may be striving to fit into our appearance-obsessed society. They may be trying to project wealth and power. Compulsive clothes shopping can signal an attempt to camouflage a negative body image. The shopper may not realize this link.
- **Perfectionism** – The overshopper may be attempting to reach unrealistically high expectations they've set for themselves or are hoping to transform themselves.

Individuals struggling with Compulsive Buying Disorder should work with a therapist or a psychiatrist—this is much more than an issue of organization. Check ShopoholicNoMore.com for additional resources.

Client Scenario Resolutions

Laura's New Condo

Two things were bothering Laura: how to best store her wardrobe and how to free up Emily's bedroom in preparation for her arrival. Over several sessions, we helped Laura significantly downsize her wardrobe.

Laura also realized that one reason she shopped so much was to soothe her raw emotions after her divorce. She had kept many items because they represented a time in her life when she was happy in her marriage. She donated several bags of clothes to local charities, including several gowns she had worn to formal events with her ex-husband many years ago.

We implemented a closet organization system that maximized her clothing storage. We created an inventory card and photographed a few of Laura's favorite outfits to help her better evaluate future purchases. To make it easier for Laura to make returns, we designated a location near the front door where she will keep any bags with returns and the accompanying receipts.

For Laura, downsizing her wardrobe was a symbol of accepting her new single life. It was the first step toward living within her means. Laura also met with a financial adviser to focus on budgeting and bringing down her credit card debt.

Michelle's New Carpet

We worked with Tom and Michelle's family over a two-month period. We worked one-on-one with Zachary and Amanda to downsize their toys and outgrown clothes. They each let go of a lot of toys they no longer wanted. Michelle was surprised how easily the children pared down their collections.

We worked with Michelle on her closet. She filled many bags with old clothing and shoes she was willing to give up. We put all of her off-season clothing in clear bins, creating more space in her closet.

Tom parted with outdated technology books, and we recycled several old computers and other obsolete electronics. We boxed up all of Tom's CDs and movies. We then tackled the LEGO™ sets and helped Tom evaluate resources for selling some of their collection. We photographed some of the displayed LEGO™ sets to preserve their memory and then broke them down. We consolidated the remaining pieces into fewer bins and moved them temporarily to a storage room.

Michelle was finally able to schedule her carpet installation!

Recap – Strategies for the Power Shopper

Clutter raises the stress-related hormone cortisol. When we reduce how much we buy or how much we have, we reduce the stress in our lives.

Here is a recap of the main topics and strategies covered in this chapter, which can help you evaluate possible purchases before actually buying.

Power Shopper Considerations	Questions to Ask Yourself
Be aware of the constant messages to buy.	• Do I like this item because I've seen ads for it on social media and in my web browser window for the past three days? • Would I even be thinking about buying this item if I wasn't at the mall or online right now? • Do I have a similar item which would perform the same duty? • If I don't buy it, will I miss not having it?
Watch for overabundance in your collection.	• Do I have space for this item? • Am I willing to donate or discard another item in my collection to make space for this one? • Does this new item fill a purpose in my collection? • Does this item have a practical use?

Watch for compromised decision-making—FOMO and decision fatigue.	• Am I only buying this because it's easy, and I am tired? • Am I buying this just because my friends said they have it? • Am I buying this because I want the lifestyle it represents? • Am I buying this because I feel I deserve to have it too?
Are we acquiring for our future?	• Am I buying based on a perceived need or an actual need? • Am I shopping for items related to something that may or may not happen? • Am I shopping for something I hope will happen, but may not actually happen?
Tech – Am I ready to get rid of my old technology?	• Is this new device a replacement or an addition to my home? Do I have the space to store it? • Am I ready and committed to fully migrate data to my new device? • Is it time to donate or recycle my old devices to make space for the new?
Is the allure of free stuff worth it?	• Is this "great deal" what is missing from my collection? • How much is enough? • Is this a duplicate item? • Will it take me a lifetime to use up what I already have?

Notes

What ideas spoke to you?

_____
_____
_____
_____

In the Words of Our Clients

The organization process was simply fantastic! Denise sat me down and helped me to realize we don't need so much stuff. She was gentle, but firm, and so down to earth. Just as we'd seen on television programs, there were Keep, Toss, and Donate piles.

I was able to get rid of so much stuff: clothes, kitchen items, books, knick-knacks, etc. I never felt pushed to do anything I was uncomfortable with or forced to get rid of something I wasn't ready to. Best of all, they took the bags with them to donate and dispose of. (Can't emphasize that last sentence enough!) The process went very quickly and eased the sense we had of being overwhelmed with getting rid of a lifetime of "stuff."

Denise was very understanding of our situation and offered many helpful suggestions which I still use today, over a year later. We had two sessions, and each time the Simplify Experts came to our home, I felt as though I could finally breathe! In those few hours, they taught me how to let go of the excess stuff that was weighing me down.

–SIMPLIFY EXPERTS CLIENT

Chapter 3

THE PAPER MAGNET

Your paper piles have reached a tipping point—literally. They are falling over. You don't open mail. You lose important documents and receipts. You are late paying bills. You fear being audited; hence, you retain all possible documentation. Your business paperwork is commingling with personal paperwork. Your file cabinets are full, so you can't use them. You print out hundreds of pages. Whenever you research something, you collect all the available pamphlets to get ideas.

Client Scenarios

Bonnie's Baskets

Bonnie is a designer. She is very social and loves to entertain in her home. For three years, when rushed before guests arrived, she put piles of mail into laundry baskets. She stored them in a closet until the closet was full, and then she moved the baskets to the garage. Eventually the garage itself became quite full, and Bonnie hired me to help her organize it.

When we came across the baskets in her garage, Bonnie wanted to recycle the contents. I asked Bonnie if I could take five minutes to look through the first laundry basket. I found documents containing personal information and account numbers. These would need to be shredded.

As we began sorting, we found unopened envelopes with year-end financial statements which needed to be filed and saved. We found unopened holiday cards, including one with a gift card! There were unopened credit card offers, catalogs, and lots of magazines. We also found an un-cashed check (for $18,000!) that Bonnie hadn't known was coming to her.

Kristin's House of Boys

Kristin first called us after her son, Alex, had asked—for the tenth time—if he could please have an allowance. On the phone, she laughed at how silly it seemed, but she felt terrible. They had talked about an allowance for years. She had promised 11-year-old Alex that she would create a savings account and transfer in an allowance once a month.

But, somehow months went by, and Kristin never got around to it. In fact, this seemingly small incident made Kristin realize just how disorganized, overwhelmed, and out of control their life had become. It was impacting the whole family—even Alex.

Kristin is a part-time dietician, and her husband, Jeff, works for a tech company. Alex and his two brothers, Aiden and Austin, play soccer, basketball, and baseball. Jeff coaches two of their teams. Kristin loves the loud, rambunctious energy the boys bring to their home. She'd much rather kick a soccer ball around than tidy up around the house. She'd rather sit through three rainy soccer games any day than stay home, pay bills, or deal with paperwork.

Jeff recently underwent back surgery, creating a bigger than usual influx of medical bills and insurance statements. Kristin took over paying bills while Jeff recovered—a chore she largely neglected. When Alex asked about his allowance, Kristin finally admitted to herself that she needed help.

When we worked together, we found that Jeff and Kristin had talked about meeting with a financial advisor, but never got around to doing it. They had an old file cabinet in the basement, but it was full of papers from before they were married.

They stored current paperwork in the closet of their little office. They usually paid their bills at the dining room table, and piled statements and documents on the buffet. They were both interested in a better way to deal with their paperwork, but needed help doing it.

Mail and Paper Pain

Few people look forward to organizing their paperwork. For one, organizing paperwork does not result in the immediate visual impact we get from organizing other items, like clothes or sports equipment.

As professional organizers, we happen to love paper! We can fly through filing cabinets with ease, pulling out the old, and filing the new. Most people find it incredibly tedious. Rarely does a client stay focused on paperwork for the duration of our standard work session. We know clients have had enough when they begin to flee the scene.

What makes paper organizing so painful?

- **It's tedious.** A ream of paper is 500 pages, and the stack isn't very tall. It takes considerable time to work through even a modest pile of mail and paperwork.
- **It's time consuming.** Some of the papers in the pile contain tasks that take a lot of time to complete.
- **It's not clear cut.** There are several categories for sorting paperwork, and it's not always obvious what must be kept and for how long. If you are not a lawyer or a tax accountant, you probably have some questions.

For many people, mail and paper are the biggest organizing pain point. It's not surprising. We may painstakingly go through a pile of paper on the desk and feel like we've accomplished nothing. After all that tedious work, the space looks no more organized.

Even if we pay bills online and don't subscribe to many publications, we still deal with mounds of paper each month. A serious backlog of paper can spring up seemingly overnight. Before we know it, there is a sizable pile of "not sure what's in there" paperwork on our kitchen counter.

A couple of weeks pass and the pile blends into the background until visitors are due to arrive—then we quickly stash that pile of "probably nothing important" paperwork in a drawer, closet, guest bedroom, or the garage.

Paper disorganization can impact more than just our finances or our credit report. It can impact the other members of your family. We lose the school picture order form, and our children miss out on having their photos taken. We miss the note about a school field trip and find ourselves scrambling to deliver a bagged lunch to school, just as the school bus is pulling away from the curb. One client missed his surgery because he lost the paperwork (not kidding!). When paperwork is not in order, the whole family can suffer.

Paper Clutter

Americans receive thousands of pieces of mail in their lifetime. Add in children's schoolwork and forms, our own documents, small business paperwork, loan documents, pamphlets, receipts, journals, etc., it's no wonder many of us feel buried in paper. When we consider all the sources of paper clutter in our homes, it becomes less surprising that many adults pay their bills late because they can't find them.

Paper Flow System

Does this sound familiar? Most days, we put the mail on the coffee table. But, other times, the pile of mail winds up on the kitchen counter, or we find it on top of the washing machine. Sometimes it's wedged under the driver's seat in the car. (Could that be where the missing prescription is?!) Pretty soon, finding paperwork in the house becomes a scavenger hunt that no one is in the mood for.

If the mail doesn't make it to the location where it will be processed, it can get sucked into the clutter vortex of our homes. If we don't file or discard invoices and bills we've already paid, they hang out on our desk indefinitely. They mingle with newly added mail. New and old paper together in piles creates confusion and frustration.

Whenever we work with clients who struggle with organizing paper, we help them set up a plan for how paper flows through their home. The paper flow system provides guidelines for efficient paper handling, including:

- The handling of mail when it comes into the home.
- Eliminating junk mail and reducing the overall volume of mail.
- Setting up a location where mail is opened and processed.
- Filing documents that need to be saved.

Mail

Let's face it: often, the things that come in the mail can be depressing. Christmas and birthday cards are fun to receive, but most of the other mail we get is not. For example, if you've been in a car accident, opening mail may remind you of all the medical procedures you've endured and how much you owe for them.

Mail can be a harsh reckoning of how much we've spent on our credit cards. Or, mail can be a reminder of our (maybe not so awesome) financial situation. If so much mail evokes unpleasant thoughts, it's no wonder the only thing we want to look at are the coupons or catalogs. Unopened mail is an incredibly common phenomenon, and, worst of all, the tide of mail just keeps coming.

One client we worked with had 14 checking accounts. She had saved hundreds of bank statements hoping to one day get around to reconciling all of them. To begin the process, she had attempted to sort the envelopes by year. Even this task was so daunting that she became paralyzed and did not know how to proceed.

We suggested that perhaps she reconcile only the past calendar year. This was a more achievable, realistic goal. She felt so incredibly relieved when she realized she had a task that she could complete. We also discussed the possibility of consolidating and reducing the number of active bank accounts she owned.

If we decrease the amount of mail that comes into our homes, then getting it organized becomes easier:

- Reduce the volume of mail you receive.
- Cancel unwanted catalogs at CatalogChoice.org.
- Opt out of offers for credit or insurance at OptOutPrescreen.com.
- Reduce physical mail by setting up autopay and having statements emailed.

One-third of the mail that arrives in our mailbox is junk. During the holiday season, that percentage grows. The average American receives 40 pounds[1] of catalogs and other junk mail each year. That's over three pounds a month.

According to a 2015 New York Times article, 11.9 billion catalogs were mailed in 2013[2]. Many people pay too much attention to junk mail. This type of mail is mostly a distraction. It's the commercial we are asked to watch before we can go back to the main attraction. When going through the mail, a glossy catalog switches our focus from *need* to *want*.

What we really *need* to focus on is delivering the mail to where it will be processed. But, when we start examining the catalog from the retail store, our focus turns to *want*. As in, I think I want this new outdoor heating lamp (according to this mailer, it's a great deal!). The rest of the mail goes in a pile on the washing machine to be dealt with later.

---

[1] Chamberlin, Brett. "The Story of Junk Mail." *The Story of Stuff Project*. 2017.Web. Jan. 2018.

[2] Ruiz, Rebecca. R. "Catalogs, After Years of Decline, Are Revamped for Changing Times." *New York Times*. 25 January 2015. Web. Jan.2018.

If we reduce how much mail we receive to begin with, and, if we can toss all the junk mail as soon as it arrives, we'll have less actual mail to open every night. The piles will never be allowed to get very high.

Lost Receipts and Found $$$

Many people are cheating themselves out of money owed to them. When we lose receipts and fail to submit reimbursements, we are robbing ourselves of potential income.

When we return from business trips, for example, receipts for client dinners, taxis, and hotels might stay in the suitcase or fall behind the nightstand. When it's time to submit an expense report, lost receipts lead to unreimbursed expenses. Even people who have company credit cards sometimes have to use cash for business purchases. When the receipt is lost, so is the money.

Similarly, insurance reimbursements for vision, dental, and mental health services may go unclaimed when the receipts are misplaced, or we forget to mail in the forms.

Multiple times a week, a member of our organizing team finds an uncashed check or cash among clients' paper piles. Some checks come in nondescript envelopes, which are easily mistaken for junk mail.

Unopened mail is a very common phenomenon. One client we worked with had boxes of unopened mail. This is simply a fact, not a judgement. This client had a demanding job, and she was a single mom; she had more demands on her time than there were hours in the day. Something had to give. The mail didn't get opened.

While sorting old mail, we came across five uncashed medical reimbursement checks totaling $350. There were no longer valid, and she wasn't excited about the prospect of calling the insurance company, possibly spending a half hour on the phone getting the checks re-issued—she didn't know when she would find the time. But, the dollar amount made it worth the effort. The lesson? It can be costly to leave mail on the table unopened. It's best to open it and start processing.

Storing Important Documents

Imagine this scenario: You've been wanting to meet with a financial planner. You want to make sure your retirement money is wisely invested. You'd like to find out whether you'll be able to pay for your child's college, and you have an old IRA that needs to be transferred. No problem, right? Just make an appointment. But, it's not that easy.

For many, what is holding them back from being able to make (and keep) that financial planner appointment is completely disorganized paperwork. They may be paralyzed by the thought of having to find that old IRA account paperwork. They may not be fully aware of how many open accounts they have or even the current balance of their accounts.

It's not just the physical paper piles that are a source of stress and anxiety. The lurking insecurity of not knowing the state of our finances and not knowing where important documents are located can cause stress and anxiety as well.

There are both short and long-term benefits to having your paperwork in order. In the short term, you'll have peace of mind and an accurate view of your savings and retirement funds. In the long-term, having your paperwork in order is a huge gift to your loved ones or the executor of your estate. Imagine passing the burden of your chaotic paperwork to your loved ones…best to tackle it now and reap all the benefits. Again, this paralyzing, overwhelming burden is not yours to bear on your own. This is tough stuff. We can help you get your paperwork ship shape.

> "Paper clutter is no more than postponed decisions."
>
> – Barbara Hemphill

Administrative Time for Your Family

To combat paper clutter, let's think of our family as a small business. We have income, expenses, taxes and bills, investments, capital improvements, and even payroll (the kids' allowance!). A successful small business needs a good bookkeeper and office manager.

We typically work with clients to reduce the overwhelming backlog of their paper clutter. Once they reach a point where they are able to manage their own paperwork with ease, then we help them determine a weekly admin time.

This dedicated time is used to address all the important administrative tasks a family has and is used to:

- Pay bills, reconcile accounts, deposit checks.
- Shred sensitive documents. See Consumer.ftc.gov for good guidelines on what documents should be shredded.
- Fill out forms for reimbursements.
- File documents to retain for your records.
- Set up health and home maintenance appointments.
- Update the family calendar.
- Set up autopay for regularly recurring bills.

Admin time might not be an activity you're likely to post about on social media, but consider how much calm it will create for you and your family to have all the paperwork in order. Undoubtedly, you will feel more relaxed and in control.

Handle Paper Once

Don't multiply your work by endlessly churning through the same piece of mail or paper documents. Aim to touch each piece of mail just once—from opening the envelope to taking the needed action to filing it. To help remember this, we use the acronym OHIO (Only Handle It Once).

When handling a piece of mail, determine if it falls into one of the following categories:

- **Actionable items.** A bill to be paid—pay it.
- **Tax-related document.** Receipts for tax deductions and year-end financial statements—file it in your current-year tax folder.

- **Reference document.** A benefits explanation or monthly investment statements—file it.

When we OHIO, we prevent paper piles from accumulating around the house, and we can enjoy the rejuvenating benefits of an organized home.

In addition to weekly admin time, once a year, in late January, make space in your filing cabinet by cleaning out last year's financial, tax, and insurance files. As you receive your year-end financial statements, file them with tax-related documents in a separate file for easy access during tax season.

Reducing Non-Mail Paper

A portion of our paper clutter doesn't come from mail at all. Piles sprout up when our children bring home paper from school (schoolwork, newsletters, forms, etc.), when we print out documents, or when we accumulate pamphlets or brochures for research.

School children bring home art projects, school forms, and homework. We want to save our children's work as a keepsake, but the amount of paper can be overwhelming. We recommend only keeping the best representation of your child's work and projects—those that best reflect who they are. Toss the daily worksheets and take photographs of hard-to-store craft projects. Purge the paper they bring home weekly, if not daily.

When doing research, reduce paper piles by choosing the three to five pamphlets you LOVE—ones that really speak to you. Sort of like being a shopper in a clothing store, by choosing only the top five items that stand out to you, you are choosing the clothing that really fits. If you've researched options for an upcoming cruise, for example, you should retain only the information regarding your final choice and recycle all the other research pamphlets and materials.

We had a client who wanted to give money to charities, but he wasn't sure which ones. He saved all charitable donation requests that he received, amounting to hundreds of pieces of mail. He and his wife wanted to decide, but they were overwhelmed by the choices.

Based on our discussion, we gleaned that he felt strongly about nature trails, theater, and public radio. We asked him whether those three causes spoke loudest to him. He agreed, and that brought the list of candidates down from 200 to three. He was okay with that. In essence, we narrowed the scope by speaking to his passions and reflecting those passions back to him.

In the same vein, keep letters or greeting cards which contain a deeply personal message or come from someone who is dear to you. Keep the cards that make your heart sing. Cards simply signed with a name should be recycled.

Client Scenario Resolutions

Bonnie's Baskets

Each time Bonnie put a basket of paper in the closet or in the garage, she believed it was only temporary. The paper would be hidden, but safe in the garage until she had time to go through it. Out of sight in the garage, Bonnie had the feeling of a temporary reset, albeit a false reset. Her desk and counter **were** temporarily clean. But, by hiding the piles, Bonnie created a future task—a task she never got around to.

After we processed all the laundry baskets in the garage, we created a paper flow system to help Bonnie control future paper piles. Even though the $18,000 check we found was old, Bonnie was able to have it reissued. It helped pay for a new car she needed. When working with clients, we have found a lot of cash and checks over the years, including one for $91,000! Bonnie was happy to get her garage back, and she was able to park her new car inside.

Kristin's House of Boys

Jeff and Kristin made an appointment with a financial advisor. Having this appointment on the calendar gave them a concrete deadline by which they needed to have certain paperwork organized. We began working in the basement. We disposed of old, unneeded documents and made room in the filing cabinet for current files.

We then moved the filing cabinet to the office for easier access. During our organizing time, one spouse worked in the office for an hour, while the other worked with a separate team organizing other parts of their home. After an hour we switched. Over a few appointments, we had not only a solid filing system, but an organized house. We then concentrated on locating and preparing documents for their impending financial advisor meeting.

Once Kristin and Jeff's paperwork was up to date, they wanted monthly appointments with an organizer to stay on top of filing and mail. They set up a bank account for each son (linked to their own account), and once a month they transfer in money for an allowance.

Recap – Strategies for the Paper Magnet

Having an organized home hinges on having organized paperwork. Remember, if you find working with paper tedious, you don't have to do it all on your own.

For most people, paper is the most challenging part of organization. The strategies in this chapter can help reduce the volume of paper coming into your home. But, if you have years of paper to go through, this may be one of those times when you would greatly benefit from professional organizing help.

Here is a recap of the main topics and strategies covered in this chapter, which can help you set up a successful paper flow process.

Paper Magnet Strategies	Strategy Details
Create a paper flow.	• Handle mail when it comes into the home. • Set up a location where mail is opened and processed. • Place incoming mail in the designated location. • Open mail and toss junk mail immediately. • File documents to be stored.
Reduce incoming mail.	• Eliminate junk mail and reduce the overall volume of mail. • Set up online bill payment and paperless statements.

Institute a weekly admin time.	• Pay bills, reconcile accounts, deposit checks. • Fill out forms for reimbursements. • File documents you'd like to retain for your records. • Remember OHIO.
Reduce non-mail paper volume.	• Reduce pamphlets and print outs, retain the top three to five brochures. • Recycle research printouts once a decision has been made. • Recycle holiday cards. • Recycle kids' schoolwork.

Notes

What ideas spoke to you?

_____
_____
_____
_____

In the Words of Our Clients

After moving twice in six years, I had about 35 boxes and bags full of papers and memorabilia. I tried to go through them by myself, but gave that up as too time consuming. I found Denise, and she loves to sort, organize, file, and toss/recycle all sorts of papers. Her services included an entirely new filing system that really works for me, replacing my old alphabetical files.

She has lots of experience and can spot which papers need to be saved and which to shred. Her service is very inclusive, and she arrives with giant bags ready to be filled with recycling or shredding. She also had a smaller bag for trash. Best of all, she takes the bags with her at the end of each work session!

She made the two-to-three hour sessions easy to take with her upbeat personality and her knowledge about filing and organizing. I learned quite a bit during our conversations. Just doing the work with her made me eager to get started reorganizing the things I have in storage—and I look forward to needing a smaller storage space in the new year.

I also have learned lots about how to better prioritize my time. I feel as if a great weight has fallen off my shoulders now that my file drawers contain only relevant and useful information. Denise also understood that there were papers which could have been shredded, but I am attached to them, so they stayed.

In other words, I did not have to give up all my past—but the papers I did give up were weighing me down mentally. Denise gets GOLD STARS in my book!

–Simplify Experts Client

Chapter 4

THE INSPIRED HOBBYIST

Your hobby projects have come to a standstill. You have so many wonderful ideas, but you just don't have enough time. Your hobbies are more than just play; your product is your legacy. You've been told you are quite skilled. You've begun many projects, but finished few. You have materials for your hobby which have gone out of style. You get inspiration and buy materials frequently.

Client Scenarios

Vivian's Scrapbook Takeover

Vivian and Robert raised three children—two who are in college and one who recently graduated. Their house, once filled with the laughter of children, now feels too big to them. They have begun discussing the idea of downsizing.

Their son, Eric, will be attending graduate school near home, and, to save rent money, Vivian and Robert agreed that he can live with them until he finishes his master's degree.

Vivian was a stay-at-home mom when her children were young, and later she became a middle school teacher. Arts and crafts were always her creative outlet. In recent years, she has started to make cards and to scrapbook, converting the guest bedroom into a craft room. She needs space to store decorative pages and supplies.

The guest bedroom closet was full of winter coats, ski clothes, luggage, and bins of keepsakes—there was no room for Vivian's craft supplies. Little by little, as her kids left for college, the stamps, a die cut machine, paper cutters, stickers, tools, ribbons, decorative pages, and albums have crept into each child's bedroom. When the kids come home for the holidays, Vivian relocates the supplies to make space, but she often loses track of where things ended up. Now, when she works, she often becomes frustrated by not being able to find what she needs.

Robert is not a big fan of Vivian's crafts. He feels that her hobby has taken over the entire house, and he doesn't like how much money is invested in it. "She shops more than she scrapbooks," he says. Also, given the volume of her supplies, he worries that Vivian will have a hard time downsizing to a smaller home.

Now that Eric is returning to live at home, Vivian and Robert need to prepare his bedroom. Vivian admits that she probably has too many supplies. But, each item for scrapbooking represents a beautiful future product, and she has a hard time deciding what to let go. Robert mentioned that Vivian hasn't completed a scrapbook project in years.

Helen's Christening Gowns

For years, Helen made gorgeous christening gowns. She loved the detailed sewing work. She had two dedicated rooms in her house where she sewed and stored a variety of lace and other material. Additionally, Helen had completed several classes on interior design. She stored thousands of samples of decorator fabrics and other interior design supplies in a third bedroom of her home.

In recent years, Helen has suffered from arthritis pain, which made some of the detailed sewing work very challenging. After several months of chronic fatigue and muscle pain, she was diagnosed with fibromyalgia. These two illnesses limited Helen's ability to make progress on any of her sewing projects. Helen felt dejected.

To make matters worse, her eye sight was worsening. Eventually, Helen conceded that she would not be able to work at the same level as in the past. She couldn't face what she knew needed to be done. She was brokenhearted about not being able to sew, but she also wanted to move on.

Hobbies Are Healthy

Hobbies allow us to express our individuality. Creating something special feels like a gift of love. Hobbies help us relax, be creative, take our mind off work or real-life issues, and stave off boredom. To work on a hobby is to focus on a pleasant activity. A hobby can be a release. It can bring beauty to an otherwise dreary day. Hobbies are a good way to learn something new and to enrich our lives.

A hobby can help us connect to other people, making us feel like a part of a group and can be something to look forward to (perhaps you're in a knitting club that meets every week). It can fulfill a need for adventure and can make our lives fuller and richer. Hobbies can give us a sense of achievement and control over our lives.

Many of us have hobbies that require gear—sometimes lots of it. We can run into serious storage issues when multiple members of the family have equipment they need to store. Photo and video equipment, musical instruments, golf clubs, skis and snowboards, and woodworking tools all can quickly create a storage shortage. Even homes with basements or attics can run out of room when trying to store multiple family members' gear and equipment. This struggle is similar to the challenge of organizing other types of household items such as toys, clothes, kitchen gadgets, etc.

For the purpose of this chapter, we will focus on craft hobbyists, who generally use indoor spaces to store their hobby materials. Sometimes, these items even take over bedrooms, dining rooms, or closets.

Craft hobbyists can be separated into two types. The recreational hobbyist is typically someone who casually picks up knitting or a craft project. The serious crafter, on the other hand, is someone whose craft defines who they are. It is their life's passion. The problems and strategies discussed in this chapter can be applied to any hobby.

Recreational Hobbyists

Visit any craft store, and there is a good chance you will be inspired to begin a new project. Many such endeavors look like one-and-done projects that can be completed in a couple of hours. The store samples ensure us, mere mortals, that we too can create something chic and beautiful. Pinterest, Etsy, and magazines also entice us with potential creative possibilities.

Any woman who came of age in the 1980s or 1990s would likely agree that Martha Stewart has had an incredible cultural impact. Martha taught us elegant ways to cook, entertain, and restore our homes. Why would we buy ready-made, when Martha showed us how to make everything from scratch? *Martha Stewart Living* magazines were gorgeous how-to guides for a graceful lifestyle.

She showed us how to make everything beautiful, be it the dinner table, a birthday party, or a craft room. Craft hobbies became a glamorous activity. Even those of us not blessed with innate creativity could make birthday party banners, holiday cards, scrapbooks, and pillows. It's so easy to get inspired and fill our storage spaces with lovely crafts, but sometimes, despite good intentions, these supplies and projects turn into clutter.

Kid Hobbyists

What if the hobbyist in the house is your child? A collector? A creator? A relentless artist? They love any creative outlet and savor every special creation. A child's "project" collection easily contributes to our clutter and storage woes.

As parents, we need to help our children manage the number of in-progress and completed projects. If their projects are taking over your closets and cluttering up common spaces, you may need to help them pick their favorites. A good way to start is to list all their different collections on a whiteboard. Then, set a reasonable boundary for the collection. The boundary can be their bedroom or a toy room—not the whole house. To help them stick to their allotted space, we like the versatility of the IKEA® Kallax cubby shelf unit. It comes in various sizes, with plenty of display space for your child's collections.

Working on this is not an easy task for a sentimental child (or a sentimental parent!). It may be easier for your child to work with a professional organizer who comes in with an objective perspective. As a parent, you set the goal you would like to achieve for the home, and we help your child meet the boundary you've set by helping them choose which items are their favorites and which ones they are ready to part with.

Some young children love to collect stuffed animals, for example, sometimes acquiring hundreds. We may help the child sort the stuffed animals by type and work with them to pare down their collection so that it fits in the allotted space. We have worked with many children, organizing all sorts of collections of crafts, LEGO™ sets, American Girl® dolls, or Breyer® horse figurines.

Good Intentions Gone Awry

Sometimes we create clutter in our homes when we take on more than we can handle. Have you ever, for example, purchased a piece of used furniture on a whim? Consider the following scenario: You were on vacation and spotted just the *perfect* table in an antique store. You were thrilled to have found this treasure. The table just needs to be refinished, and it will be perfect!

But, now that table sits in the garage, where it has been for the past two years. You thought refinishing it would be super easy. You even watched some videos about it. You bought all the supplies, and when it came time to do it, you found that it was much harder than it seemed at first. The smells from the solvents made you feel nauseous, and it was hard work, so you put the project on hold.

Maybe you'd try it again in the summer when you could work outside, and the solvent fumes wouldn't be an issue. But, summer came, and other activities took priority. The table was once again forgotten. Now, you only think of it when the weather is bad, and you wish you could park in your garage. This happens to all of us at some point. Our plans and intentions go a bit awry.

This is a common scenario, and it doesn't only happen with antique furniture projects. Sometimes, we invest in something (music recording equipment or a fancy sewing machine), and it turns out, for whatever reason, that it's not for us. We don't like it as much as we thought we would.

We may be holding on to it because of guilt. We may be hoping that in some distant future this item will fit our life better. It is perfectly okay to let this item go—whatever it may be and no matter how expensive it was. In business, it's called a sunk cost. Instead of fretting, embrace the thought of the clear open space and how relaxing that space will be.

Serious Crafters

Then, there are those of us who (without Martha's help) have an innate talent to make quilts, knit, or sew. You know who you are! You truly love your craft. Others have praised your talent. You invest your time, money, and creative energy into your art. The prospect of beginning something beautiful and new excites you.

You may have several projects going simultaneously. Sometimes, for a variety of reasons, you don't complete a project. Time may pass, and perhaps you start another project and that one stalls too. You may reach a point where you aren't seeing much progress on any of your current projects.

You might walk by an abandoned project in your home and feel frustrated, overwhelmed, and discouraged. Buying materials for your hobby still excites you, but mostly you feel stuck. These projects often take up a lot of space in your home and may cause friction in your household.

We've seen this scenario with many clients. While the picture may seem bleak, there is a remedy. A painter needs her paints and brushes by her side, not scattered across the house. When your hobby materials are organized, using the strategies in this chapter, you'll be effective at your work again. Once organized, you'll have a clear picture of your inventory of materials as well as the location and status of all your in-progress projects. There will be nothing stopping you. The love and passion for your hobby will blossom once again. You'll be amazed at how quickly this will happen for you.

Your Hobby—Your Collection

When you begin to invest in supplies for a hobby, you begin a collection. While some collect stamps or dolls, others may be building a collection of catalogs, tools, materials, and supplies needed for their hobby. Such a collection can quickly grow to exceed the available storage space in your home. It happens easily.

We all have a natural inclination to purchase things that inspire us. To work on something beautiful is therapeutic and meditative—who wouldn't love that? Inspiration gives us a hopeful feeling, and there are so many inspiring items to buy—it's really easy to buy too much.

Overshopping for hobby materials can also be related to the following causes:

- You want to fulfill your role as a talented creator.
- You have so many ideas!
- You see potential in all kinds of materials.
- Your friends have asked you to create items for them, and you don't want to let them down.
- You belong to a club that sells monthly craft kits.

How Many Projects?

How many projects can you comfortably work on at the same time? Let's ask that question another way. Does the current level of control you have over your projects allow you to carry out your hobby in the way you imagined?

For most individuals, it's best to limit active projects to a number that can be counted on one hand. Five or more and you may have too little time available to keep momentum going toward project completion.

We once helped a client narrow her projects to 50. You read that right—narrow to 50! She was a quilter and loved to make items for her family, but her collection had overtaken her home. We downsized hundreds of pounds of fabric.

Two years later, when she hadn't made headway on most of the 50 projects, we worked together again, narrowing the project list to 25. This number is, of course, still very high, but considering where she started, this was an immense achievement. This client was a prolific quilter and incredibly generous with her beautiful creations. Her grandchildren have nearly 40 of her quilts to cherish for years to come.

Define Top Projects

There is great allure to starting a new project, and excitement when a project is finished. But, the middle can be hard, and this is where most people stall. At this juncture, it's tempting to put the project down for a bit, take a break, and work on something else. When this happens repeatedly, half-finished projects begin to create clutter in the hobby space (or the entire house!).

To keep a pulse on each in-progress project, it helps to get visual. Use a whiteboard or create a project spreadsheet to track your progress. We've included an example of a project spreadsheet below.

In the spreadsheet document, list all in-progress projects and assign a numerical priority to each. Then, sort the projects according to priority and put materials for each project into its own bin. Finally, write the name of the project and the priority number on each bin. If you have too many projects, this may feel overwhelming. Remember, you don't have to tackle this on your own. Two sets of hands are better than one, and we would love to offer ours to help!

Sample Project Spreadsheet

Project Number	Project Name	Priority	% Complete	Date Due	Comments
1					
2					
3					
4					
5					

How Important Is the Project?

The project list may be lengthy. To make progress, we need to allocate dedicated time each week to work on the top-priority projects. Sometimes, there may be extenuating circumstances (such as an illness, vacation, or business trip) that may keep us from working on a project. That's just life. Other times, though, you may find you've missed your deadline over and over again. This might be a sign that this project isn't as important to you as others. That's perfectly okay. You should ask yourself if keeping this project on the top five list still feels authentic?

Given that you have existing projects under way, when considering whether to add a new project, ask yourself whether you will be able to work on it in the next 12 months. If the answer is NO, for any reason (illness, new job, new baby, or you are already working on several projects), then it's best not to allocate the project any space, time, or supplies.

Some people find it difficult to decide when a project is no longer important to them. They feel that they "should" complete the project. This feeling can be attributed to any number of reasons. But when we hear that "should" voice in our heads, it's not necessarily our own voice speaking to us, but rather, our interpretation of someone else's expectations of us.

The best course of action is to try to turn off that voice and focus on the big picture—making physical and emotional space so that you are able to make progress on your top most important projects. You will immediately notice how empowering it feels to change your mindset from "I probably should work on these…" to "I choose to work on this project…"

Give It a Deadline

Now that you have a list of all the projects, you can assign a due date for each. This can be tricky. Baby gifts have a due date attached. Christmas stockings also have a built-in due date. Other projects need an arbitrary (but realistic) deadline to keep the momentum going. Choose a deadline that seems reasonable to you. (See the Overburdened Employee chapter for more momentum building strategies.)

Create a Workspace

Sometimes our projects come to a standstill because our workspace is wrong. If a hobby is truly important, then it deserves a set location, proper desk or table, dedicated storage, and appropriate lighting. What aspects of your workspace could be derailing you?

- Do you need space to work in a group?
- Is your workspace set up ergonomically? Are your sewing machine and ironing board at the correct height?
- Do you have the tools you need at each workstation?

By the same token, the hobby work should only reside in its designated space. When we take over the dining room table and the project stays there for weeks, the result may be that the family is regularly eating dinners on the couch. It tells family members that the project is more important than they are—the family, after all, got kicked out of the dining room. It also sends the message that it's okay to leave their stuff all over the place. Either way you look at it, projects shouldn't create clutter in the common areas of the home.

A Stash or a SABLE?

Our hobby materials are our "stash"—everything we need to do our craft. If the stash evolves into a "SABLE" then we have a volume problem. SABLE stands for <u>S</u>tash <u>A</u>ccumulated <u>B</u>eyond <u>L</u>ife <u>E</u>xpectancy.

Some hobbyists accumulate so much, they'd have to live to be 200 to use it all. No doubt, such a large collection is impacting the entire home. Often multiple rooms of homes are rendered unusable for their intended purpose because they've become storage.

Once you've established which projects are truly the most important (hopefully no more than five at a time), then it's time to tackle the SABLE. Keep these strategies in mind to avoid accruing too much material:

- Bring the volume of supplies down only to the amount needed for current projects.
- Define the boundary for space allocated to the hobby.
- Scale back extras, dispose of out-of-style materials, and make it fit the allotted space.

Does this sound like an impossible project? If you have a sizeable SABLE, it may be difficult to make significant headway on your own. But, in three hours working with a professional organizer, you will complete what would take you ten plus hours working solo.

Bless It on to Someone Else

What does it mean to "bless it on to someone else"? It means that any project which has stopped being fun might be a blessing for someone else out there. It means, it's okay to give up on something if it has "expired for you." If a project you've started, turns out NOT to be what you thought—for whatever reason—it's okay to let it go.

You don't need to finish it … you can bless it on to someone else. No need to carry around the emotional weight of unfinished projects. Letting go brings tremendous relief. Some groups hold bazaars, and donated items (even half-finished) garner money for a good cause. Sometimes, craft materials can go directly to a program, like Project Linus which helps veterans battling PTSD or to prisons where they may be used for rehabilitation classes.

It is also perfectly okay to let someone else help you with your project. If, for example, your eyesight isn't great (perhaps you're having trouble threading the needle), and it becomes too difficult to handle the fine details, let someone else do that portion of the job. If you've retired a "mostly finished project," sometimes you can pay people to finish them for you. Connect with a local guild to find these folks.

> "Certain things catch your eye, but pursue only those that capture the heart."
>
> – Ancient Indian Proverb

Client Scenario Resolutions

Vivian's Scrapbook Takeover

When we worked with Vivian, she saw her entire collection for the first time in years. In Vivian's home, the guest bedroom had been her craft room, but it still had a queen bed. The room had been overfull for years, so no one had used this bed. Whenever guests came, they slept in one of the kids' rooms.

We took out the queen bed. We relocated the winter coats, luggage, and ski equipment that filled the closet. Now this room was a blank canvas, ready for a transformation into a craft room. The closet was converted to provide better storage space. We inventoried Vivian's in-progress projects, input them into the spreadsheet, and prioritized them. We stored Vivian's projects and extra supplies in clear plastic bins on new shelves in her overhauled craft room.

During this process, Vivian found a lot of items she had long forgotten, most of which no longer fit her plans. Having the newly-created project list there in the room provided a nice accountability.

By the end of the process, she had donated an astounding 20 large bins of scrapbooking materials to the Boys and Girls Club, a Senior Center, and Tree House, an organization that supports foster families.

Now that a large work table fit into the room, Vivian would no longer need to use the dining table to work. Vivian was able to find and identify her top projects. She was ready to finish her scrapbooks.

The couple also realized that to downsize to a smaller house they would need to declutter each of the children's bedrooms. Since their kids were away at college, Robert and Vivian would take the next two years to work with their kids over holiday breaks, slowly cleaning out ancient toys and keepsakes, and packing up in preparation for the move.

Helen's Christening Gowns

For Helen, who had arthritis and fibromyalgia, we took time, working at her pace, to downsize her collection of fabrics. We helped her create a priority project list and placed her projects in small totes that were easy for her to move. She decided to part with 10 carloads of fabric and lace, as well as all of her interior decorator samples. When we finished she asked that we check in by phone every month.

Helen continued to make progress, knowing we would call for updates about her projects. Sometimes, she sent me photos of her completed work. Her progress was slower than in the past, but still stunning.

Recap – Strategies for the Inspired Hobbyist

Whether you are a recreational hobbyist or a serious crafter, your hobbies should bring joy to your day. If the number of projects and the amount of materials thwarts that joy, use the strategies in this chapter to organize your hobby space and your projects to get that joy back.

Get help if you need to declutter a vast collection, or if you want to work with someone to prioritize and organize your projects. Working alone on your hobby is restorative, but organizing your hobby space and materials is best accomplished with two sets of hands.

Here is a recap of the main topics and strategies covered in this chapter, which can help you approach a reorganization of your hobby projects.

Inspired Hobbyist Strategies	Strategy Details
Organize your projects.	• Take inventory of all your projects. • Write down and name all the projects. • Define your top-priority projects. • Limit the number of projects you are actively working on and target the top five. • Give your projects a deadline. • Let the project go if it has expired for you. • Get help completing difficult parts of projects.

Organize your hobby space.
- Inventory your collection of materials to determine if you have a stash or a SABLE.
- Bring down the volume of your supplies to support only current projects.
- Shop for current projects only.
- Limit supplies to allocated space.
- Create a workspace that supports your project needs.
- Work in your dedicated workspace.

Notes

What ideas spoke to you?

_____

_____

_____

_____

In the Words of Our Clients

If I could give more than 5 stars I would. A few months ago, I decided I wanted to begin painting again. I wanted to set up my art studio, but I was overwhelmed and didn't know where to start.

All of my paints and canvases were buried in the garage and in various closets. I needed help to find everything and organize it. I couldn't believe how the volume of stuff was creating such blockage.

I called Simplify Experts, and they were great. I could have never finished alone what took them just a matter of days. They were efficient, compassionate, and had such great ideas.

Now that I am settled in my new studio, I can focus on my art again. I feel creative again. I can get to my canvases. I am painting again! We used a shelving unit for my paints...I can see it all.

I am more selective about what I keep for inspiration. I can honestly say that I would not be where I am today if they hadn't helped me.

–Simplify Experts Client

Chapter 5

THE CAREGIVER

Everything else must take a backseat to caregiving. You are the primary caregiver to many. You've been able to stay organized in the past, but now you use all your time and energy caring for others. It's impossible to keep up. Family relationships are strained. You experience constant pressure. You have no time for yourself.

Client Scenarios

Shelly's Special Needs

Shelly and Tim described their son as spirited and precocious—all boy. Little Jack's personality is different than that of his older sisters, who played quietly, bordering on being shy. Shelly figured all boys must be like this.

In elementary school, Jack made frequent visits to the principal's office, sometimes just to cool off. Jack attended occupational therapy. He and his sisters struggled with asthma and other allergies, with frequent visits to an allergy specialist. In third grade, an IEP (Individualized Educational Plan) helped ease some of Jack's classroom issues. In fourth grade, Jack really began to struggle in class, and his parents decided to pursue a psychiatric evaluation. Jack was diagnosed with anxiety, ADHD (Attention Deficit Hyperactivity Disorder), and ODD (Oppositional Defiant Disorder).

Tim travels for work two weeks each month. Although Shelly stays at home with the children, managing everything on her own with three separate kids' schedules and Jack's extra appointments was taking a toll. After-school activities, appointments, homework battles, and bedtime were often a struggle, leaving Shelly depleted. Many nights by 10:30 p.m., she would collapse into bed, emotionally and physically exhausted.

Their home was emblematic of their frenetic life. Shelly was fighting an uphill battle, falling behind on housework, bills, and personal health appointments. Two years ago, Tim began a project to replace the baseboards in their house, but he has completed only half of the house.

A cleaning service helps, but creates anxiety for Shelly, who tries to pick up around the house on the day the cleaners come. Many times, Shelly grabs a bag, fills it with whatever is laying around and stows it in a closet, just to get the house reasonably ready to be cleaned.

She is frustrated that the kids' rooms are always littered with clothes and toys, and that their home improvement projects have come to a standstill. Shelly wants us to help her calm the chaos in her home and wants to have time for self-care.

Kathleen's Time to Triage

Kathleen is a physician, working full-time at the hospital. She and Jim have three children. Their oldest daughter, Lexi, struggles with anxiety, and Lexi's younger sisters, who are twins, were diagnosed with ADHD in the fourth grade. All three kids have IEPs at school. Over the past three years, they have changed schools twice as Kathleen tries to find the best fit. Lexi and her sisters share a bedroom. Their bedroom floor is 18-inches-deep with clothes.

Jim's father has Parkinson's disease and needs a lot of help. Jim does most of the caregiving. He drives his father to all of his doctor's appointments, which takes about five hours each week. Jim's extended family call him to find out how grandpa is doing. Jim helps his father with bills and other household tasks, but Jim struggles with organization and time management. He confides that he, too, may have ADHD. Jim's favorite hobby is breeding dogs. Currently, they have three adult dogs and nine puppies, bringing a lot of chaotic energy to the house.

Life at home is challenging. When Kathleen gets home from work, she goes into triage mode, trying to resolve the most urgent needs of the family. She has no time or energy to plan her next day or put things away. And, the cleaners, kids, and Jim, all put things away in different locations (or not at all), so whenever Kathleen is looking for something, she frequently can't find it and becomes incredibly frustrated.

Just keeping up with laundry is a hardship. There are piles of unwashed clothes on the floor of the laundry room (along with hundreds of unmatched orphan socks). To top things off, last month, the chaos in their life caused Kathleen to forget a parent-teacher conference. She is at her wits end. Kathleen and Jim would like to create a calmer home environment for their children, especially to ease Lexi's anxiety.

> **To the world you may be one person; but to one person you may be the world.**
>
> – Dr. Seuss

Demands on Caregivers

You may be cruising along through life when an unexpected event flips everything upside down. Daily life takes a backseat while you care for an ill family member, care for elderly parents, or raise a special needs child. These demands mean that you have even less time to organize your life, but they also mean that you have an even greater need for a well-organized life.

This generation of seniors is relatively healthier and is expected to live longer than any previous generations. Additionally, many in our generation married and had children later in life than our predecessors. As a result, many of us must deal with caring for both very young children and elderly or ill parents at the same time. You may spend many hours each week tending to the needs of others.

Taking care of children with special needs requires a lot of extra time and effort. You may be juggling recurring doctor appointments, hospital visits, specialist appointments, medical tests, physical therapy, tutoring, speech therapy, social skills playgroup, and school accommodations meetings—all while working and parenting your other children.

Caregiving can sap your physical and emotional energy. If being organized doesn't come easily, then keeping a home calm when time is at such a premium is very challenging. When someone is the main caregiver—a "first responder"—they can't afford any extra chaos. This is when you would benefit most from a calm and peaceful environment.

You spend valuable emotional and physical energy caring for others, sometimes at the expense of your own needs. Caregivers often take 100-percent ownership of another individual's care and may often be very hard on themselves. They expect to be able to manage everything and do it perfectly. They may resist help from others. Additionally, being a caregiver can create new strains on relationships, adding to the stress. Sometimes family dynamics shift, and relationships with siblings and other family change. As hard as it may be, caregivers need to let go of some of the control and ask for help.

Don't be Afraid to Delegate

You can't pour from an empty cup. Take care of yourself first. Caregivers are inundated with responsibilities, testing the limits of their bandwidth. It is critical to defer or eliminate any non-essential activities or tasks. This is not a good time to agree to serve on the board of the PTA or take on extra responsibilities at work. This is a time when you as a caregiver need help.

Delegate as many tasks as possible. Think about the areas of your life where you don't have to be the main caregiver. Some family members may even surprise you as they rise to the occasion in unexpected ways. Your spouse may find that they have hidden laundry skills, for example, or you may have a budding chef among your teens who is able to take over dinner duty!

There are several ways to simplify grocery shopping and meal preparation. Have groceries delivered or take advantage of grocery stores with curbside pickup programs. Kroger and Walmart, among other retailers, provide these programs. Or, sign up for one of the home meal delivery services as an alternative to home-cooked meals. When cooking, always make extra for left-overs and for the freezer.

We have helped many clients put systems in place that make life easier during intensely stressful caregiving times. We have worked with clients who hire us to open their mail, pay their bills, and do their filing. We have created checklists to help kids get ready to go to school or to remind them what needs to be done after school, helping them become more autonomous. We have worked with clients on email templates specifying what they want to communicate to family. We have even decorated clients' homes for holidays!

Letting Others Help

Perhaps you can coordinate all the care, but assign family members specific tasks. Adding a weekly one-hour family meeting where tasks are delegated can create three hours of free time for you. When delegating tasks to others, be clear about the timeframe and expectations of the end result. Have the person responsible repeat back or clarify those expectations with you.

Once you give very clear, specific instructions, don't micromanage. Helpers may have a different methodology; it doesn't matter how they get there, as long as they meet the end goal.

Here are some strategies to make sure helpers can share the load of responsibilities:

- Create a list of every task and chore that needs to be completed at the patient's home and assign these chores to family members.
- Use a shared online family calendar as a communication tool to keep everyone apprised of appointments and tasks.
- Use a shared online grocery list to share shopping duties.
- Consider selecting one person to be on point to communicate information to the rest of the family. Distribute a list of phone numbers of family members and other helpers.

Organize Medical Information

Having medical information organized in a central location guarantees you always have all the important documents and information available. We suggest creating a designated binder for all healthcare paperwork. This binder will help simplify caregiving for you and other helpers by creating a central location for copies of medical histories, notes, and all medical provider contact information.

It will be the place where you keep important information and documents together and will enable you to be more proactive with patient care, since the patient's medical information will be easily accessible.

Here's a list of what the binder should include:

- **Medical history** – Download a medical history template, fill it out, and bring copies to every new medical provider appointment.
- **Appointment notes** – Take notes during appointments and keep a list of everything that's happened since the last appointment. Add any questions you might have for providers.
- **Prescription list** – Detail every medication being taken and add relevant notes. Request prescriptions for a 90-day supply of medications and coordinate the dates for prescription refills of meds to minimize trips to the pharmacy. Many insurance plans also offer mail-order options for medications, which can save even more time.
- **Daily journal** – Keep a daily journal at the patient's home and ask all caregivers to document the events relating to your loved one. This

can be a permanent record, where you'll be able to see trends and look back to check when certain events occurred. This can also be a place to collect questions for doctors as well as a helpful tool later when you need to review what the doctor or surgeon said.

Self-Care

Taking time to replenish is critical. There is nothing selfish about making sure you take care of yourself when you are taking care of others. Respite care is critical for your well-being.

Schedule regular time for self-care, even if only a few minutes each day. Block out the time–if it is on the calendar you are more likely to make it happen! When you have nothing in your reserves, you are of no benefit to anyone, and if you go down the ship sinks. This is the time to be especially kind to yourself. Take a nap. A quick twenty-minute of rest in the afternoon goes a long way.

Other suggestions:

- Protect your relationship with your spouse by finding time to talk and spend time together.
- Consider joining a regular support group.
- Schedule regular appointments with a therapist.
- Ask a friend to check in with you periodically.
- Schedule exercise dates with a friend or your spouse.
- Spend one-on-one time with each child, doing a special activity together.

During trying times, it is critical to have an awareness of your limits. You can only carry the world on your back for so long. You deserve a break. Symptoms such as unusual sleeplessness, anxiety, depression, irritability, social withdrawal, anger, poor concentration, or new health problems can be a sign of caregiver stress or burnout, and a signal that it's time to get help. For example, you may need to hire someone from a professional nursing agency or a geriatric care manager to help coordinate care. Just as a CPA helps manage your taxes, a care manager can be a huge asset when navigating the complexities of the healthcare system.

Client Scenario Resolutions

Shelly's Special Needs

To ease Shelly's caregiving duties, we worked to take some things off her plate. We prioritized all the after-school appointments and activities and counted how many hours these required. To give the kids more downtime at home, Shelly decided they would drop one after-school club. This change freed up four hours each week, resulting in less driving time and more relaxation time at home.

We downsized old toys and created room to put away toys in the kids' closets. We stored some toys in the attic. Shelly will rotate toys out periodically, keeping the volume down and making daily pickup faster. Twice a week, Shelly hires a mother's helper to play with the kids and to help her stay on top of household chores. During this time Shelly takes a walk with a friend.

We created a paper flow (see the Paper Magnet chapter), setting up automatic bill pay and email delivery of many items, such as monthly financial statements. We arranged for Tim and Shelly to begin spending one hour each Sunday on bills, weekly calendar scheduling, and planning. These changes lowered Shelly's stress about unpaid bills and allowed them to plan when Tim could help with childcare.

Tim agreed to hire a handyman to finish the baseboard project. On Saturdays, Shelly now attends a yoga class; she loves the exercise and loves that it lowers her stress. She is still very busy, but taking these small steps has helped her gain a little more control. We agreed to check in after three months to see what additional steps could be taken to relieve Shelly's stress.

Kathleen's Time to Triage

When we worked with Kathleen, we began in the kids' rooms. Kathleen's goal was to get the floors cleared. We donated a lot of old toys and clothes they had outgrown. Lexi was thrilled to have a more grownup bedroom without all of the baby toys in it. We helped the kids practice putting their clothes and toys away. And Kathleen was thrilled to be rid of the clutter!

We decluttered the entire kitchen, tossing expired food items. Kathleen donated many unused kitchen gadgets, which freed up space in the cabinets. We labeled where every item belonged to make it easier for the housecleaners and family members to return items to where they belong.

We set up a laundry system. We added a shelving unit in the laundry room, creating space for the laundry baskets and keeping the floor free of laundry piles. Each family member got their own laundry basket (labeled with their name), and each is responsible for putting away their own laundry. We helped the kids learn how to take a load of laundry and put it away in their bedroom. We discarded hundreds of orphan socks, and Kathleen purchased new, single-color socks that would be easy to pair up once washed.

We worked on time management skills with both Kathleen and Jim, helping them sync calendars and employ better communication about appointments. We implemented online bill pay, making it easier for Jim to stay on top of the bills. We downsized unneeded old paperwork and set up a filing system that significantly reduced clutter in the office. Kathleen was excited to be able to use her desk again for checking email in the evenings.

Kathleen and Jim both agreed that having a professional organizer visit once a month would help them stay caught up. The organizer would declutter and help with filing and mail (both their own and grandpa's).

Jim realized he needed as much time as possible to care for his father, so he is taking a temporary break from breeding dogs. They found homes for all the puppies. Jim hired a dog walking service to exercise their three remaining dogs during the day, freeing him up a bit more to help take care of his father.

Recap – Strategies for The Caregiver

Caregivers may benefit more than anyone else from the organizing strategies in this book, yet they often have the least amount of time and energy to implement them. Allow others to help! Using the strategies in this chapter, you can gain back valuable time and reduce the overwhelming stress that caregiving can cause.

Here is a recap of the main topics and strategies covered in this chapter that can help you manage the many demands of being a caregiver.

Caregiver Strategies	Strategy Details
Let others help.	• Communicate task goals and timeline clearly.
	• Set up regular family meetings.
	• Delegate tasks to family members and helpers.
	• Defer tasks and activities to ease your load.
	• Eliminate nonessential tasks and activities.
	• Hire helpers to simplify routine and complete your household tasks.

Prioritize self-care.	<ul><li>Schedule both rest and exercise.</li><li>Join a support group or utilize a therapist.</li><li>Nourish your relationships with your spouse and children.</li><li>Know your limits.</li></ul>

Notes

What ideas spoke to you?

___
___
___
___

In the Words of Our Clients

If I could, I would rate this company as an "A+" in every category. Before contracting their service, I was overwhelmed as I sorted through papers and clutter belonging to my mom as well as my husband and myself.

My mom moved in a few years ago with personal items, volumes of photos, and genealogy research. This was added to our own clutter—the result of 45 years of marriage and raising three kids. Unfortunately, almost a year and a half ago, both my Mom and my husband were required to enter assisted living within the same month. The past year has been incredibly stressful, which has made it impossible for me to keep on top of paperwork—some of which needs to be maintained, and some just needs to be shredded or tossed.

On day one of initial triage, Pam and Paula did an outstanding job keeping focused (and keeping me focused). After the first day, I could not have been more pleased. One of the big projects was to reduce the amount of holiday decorations that had been sitting in nice plastic bins, but had not been used for a long time. Between day one and day two, our adult children came by to help me winnow down and sort things into keep and don't keep piles.

There were tons of professional engineering books that belonged to my husband, and we all agreed the best decision was to donate. The next task was deciding what to do with our large collection of historical nonfiction and fiction books. The kids picked what they wanted, and the rest was donated. I had already purged a couple of clothes closets and bagged clothing prior to their arrival on the first day, but, with the kids help, was able to set aside a few more bags and clear additional closet shelves.

Day two was final triage. With the kids' help, I had collected many bags of donation items, and Pam and Paula immediately put those items in their vans. My overall goal was to reorganize two unused bedrooms and to declutter our neglected family room. Not only did the project go as planned, but they were so efficient that we still had 30 minutes left on the clock. A long neglected 'cubby closet' was cleared of clutter, and we added more items to the donate, keep, and trash bags.

So much more was decluttered and reorganized than I had ever imagined could be accomplished in six hours. I said good-bye to a total of four boxes worth of shredding and four carloads of donations. Big bonus: I can now find my sewing machine again!

I count these two ladies as angels among us, who walk the Earth disguised as people. My thanks is not deep enough. I will use this company again when it is time to declutter the garage, and I highly recommend their services to anyone.

–SIMPLIFY EXPERTS CLIENT

Chapter 6

THE EASILY DISTRACTED

The demands on your time are endless. Your to-do list never gets done. You are only able to put out the fires. Constant distractions break your focus! When a task is hard, and you can't bear it, you procrastinate, choosing to do something fun instead. Sometimes, you just can't stick to the priorities. You commonly think to yourself, where has all the time gone?

Client Scenarios

Alicia's Troublesome Tasks

Alicia, her husband Adam, and their young son rent a small house in Seattle. Adam recently changed jobs, and as a result, the family is enrolled in a new health insurance plan. When their son, Nathan, needed ear tube surgery, Alicia forgot to provide the new insurance information to the healthcare provider. The ear tube surgery treatments were rejected by the no-longer-valid insurance plan, resulting in a slew of mail from both the insurance carrier and the healthcare providers. Alicia and Adam were overwhelmed and stopped opening the bills. A few weeks later, they began receiving notices from collections agencies.

Alicia is a busy mom who runs a hairstyling business from home. She loves hair care products and struggles to find storage for her products in their small home.

Alicia feels like she frequently runs out of time to accomplish things, especially when it comes to household tasks. By the time she finishes with her last client and picks up Nathan from the babysitter, it's time to make dinner and put Nathan to bed. On the weekends, Alicia and Adam like to spend the day with Nathan at a museum or park. Grocery shopping, making meals, paying bills, and other household tasks are often done at the last minute or not at all.

Alicia and Adam would like to buy a home soon. In order to do that, they need to clear up the insurance bill situation and meet with a financial advisor to evaluate their home financing options. They contacted us to get help with time management and to declutter and better store Alicia's hair care products.

Cindy's Anxious Mornings

Cindy and Todd live outside of Seattle. Cindy loves her corporate job downtown. Todd works for a company based in Houston. He travels to Texas every Monday and returns Friday afternoon. They have three daughters. The older two, Amanda and Chloe, attend a private school in Seattle. The youngest, Samantha, attends a preschool near their home. Cindy employs a part-time nanny to pick up Samantha from school and play with her until she and the other girls come home in the evening.

Weekdays are all about trying to get everyone to school and then getting to work on time. The preschool charges a penalty for late drop off and late pickup, and Cindy has had to pay this penalty so frequently that she considers it a part of the preschool tuition. She is doing the best she can, but sometimes that means they are late. She finds herself being short with her girls during the anxiety-ridden morning commutes. After preschool drop off, Cindy battles the traffic into Seattle.

The family spends weekends doing fun activities together. This family time is very important to them because it's the only time Todd gets to see the kids. But, as a result, home management tasks and chores don't get done and are left for Cindy to get done in the evenings or during work hours.

Cindy is behind on errands, paperwork, house projects, and hasn't had time to plan summer camps for the kids. If she thinks about all she needs to get done, her head spins. They can never catch up on laundry, even when the nanny washes and folds some of the clothes during the week. Amanda and Chloe complain that they don't have the clothes they need to get ready for school.

Chloe and Amanda love shopping with their grandma. Grandma also buys the girls clothes and accessories when the girls are not with her to choose. Sometimes these clothes are not the right style, so they don't get worn. Both girls' rooms are a mess of clean and dirty clothes on the floor, frustrating Todd and Cindy.

Cindy reached out to us for assistance. She lamented that they often forget to empty the mailbox and sometimes miss important paperwork. Her demanding daily schedule takes everything out of her, including her sense of control over her week. She feels overwhelmed and is always behind schedule. She often works at night after the kids have gone to bed, but she says she is not very productive at that time of day. Cindy is not sure how she can fit in all her responsibilities and still feel like she is good mother to her children.

Her daughter Amanda missed a school field trip because Cindy didn't turn in the required school forms. Cindy got a teary phone call from Amanda, who was the only one in her class who had to stay behind while everyone else enjoyed the class trip.

Where Does the Time Go?

Why do so many people struggle with time management? Now, more than ever, our workday is interwoven with our personal time, to the point that many of us are never truly "off." The incoming tide of communication—data, news, marketing messages, and opinions—creates endless distractions. For many people, time just disappears, and they struggle to make a plan and stick to it. If this sounds like your life, don't worry. You are not alone! With some help, a bit of awareness, and effective strategies, it is possible to cut through the noise.

24/7 Workday

Americans work a lot of hours. A recent survey said, 18 percent of fully employed Americans work over 60 per hours a week[3]. We start checking work email while we brush our teeth in the morning. Many of us take our work home with us, both because we need to and because technology allows us to.

Even for those of us who are wizards at time management, available time for non-work activities is in short supply. Non-work time is often taken up by our children's extracurricular activities, sports and hobbies, or spent caring for family members. When evening comes, we have little energy, willpower, appetite—whatever you want to call it—for "more work." We collapse on the couch and binge watch our favorite TV show. Often, we choose what we want to do over what we need to do. What we *need* to do in those tired evening moments is to plan the next day, open the mail, and pick up around the house. But when you have no energy left, this is very hard to do.

> **Time is what we want most but what we use worst.**
>
> -William Penn

---

[3] McGregor, Jena. "The average workweek is now 47 hours." *The Washington Post.* 2 September 2014. Web. Jan. 2018.

Division of Labor

What else keeps us from being able to maximize our time? Women are still handling more of the housework and child care duties than men, according to a 2017 report by the US Bureau of Labor Statistics[4].

Put another way, one of the many reasons we feel overwhelmed is that we aren't getting the help we need at home from our partners. If your current division of labor works for you and your family, that's wonderful. If, on the other hand, you are not being supported, you are feeling overwhelmed, or some tasks better fit your partner's skill set, then a conversation might be in order.

It may be a conversation you've already had. It is a tricky subject to navigate, but nevertheless a conversation worth having. To get engagement from your partner, it's often helpful to create visual awareness of all the tasks that need to be done by posting a list of tasks on the refrigerator or a whiteboard. Another helpful strategy is to hold a family meeting and approach these tasks like a team.

At your family meeting, ask these questions:

- How can we tackle these projects?
- Are we willing to allocate the time to get this task done? How will that work?
- Do we need to hire someone to do this for us?

Distractions

How are we supposed to get anything done with so many distractions? Distractions impact all of us. We are frequently doing several things at once. It seems like there are always multiple people who need something from us, all at once. In addition to your boss, spouse, and children, we often have multiple devices constantly vying for our attention.

---

4   ATUS, Staff. "American Time Use Survey." Washington D.C.: Bureau of Labor Statistics. 2017.Web. Jan. 2018. https://www.bls.gov/tus/

Distractions and interruptions derail and frustrate even the most organized human beings out there. It's useful to think about what makes it difficult for you specifically to focus and be productive. Is it the distraction of a phone beeping with social media updates? A schedule full of meetings without any time to answer emails? Identifying the cause of your distractions gives you the power to change it. We can adjust and adapt to minimize the impact these distractions have on our day. We can also use strategies to maximize and focus our time.

In this chapter, we will discuss three elements which detract from productivity: time fluidity, decision fatigue and impulsivity. Then, we will discuss how to improve daily functionality with specific planning tools.

Time Fluidity

Our world demands absolute efficiency, but let's face it, that is not usually realistic. We can learn and follow good time management habits, but it's important to realize that we are not perfect. Even when we try our best, we will still sometimes fall short.

Time plays tricks on us. Have you heard yourself say, "It will only take 15 minutes." And then, when you look at the time, you realize it's been an hour. We've all experienced this at one point or another. Time slips away when we don't want it to.

For many people, including those with Attention Deficit Hyperactivity Disorder (ADHD), perception of time is tricky. For those with ADHD brain chemistry, Dr. Ned Hallowell[5] describes the perception of time as either "now" or "not now." If a task is urgently required right now, then we can focus. But, if a task is due at some point in the future, it's almost as if it doesn't exist at all.

It's really challenging to cope with modern-day demands on time when your brain is wired this way. Becoming aware of time, learning to *see time*

---

5   Hallowell, Edward, M. "ADHD and Time." *Dr. Hallowell's Blog.* 2 March 2018. Web. Feb. 2018. http://www.drhallowell.com/adhd-and-time-2/

pass is critical. We recommend adding analog clocks to any space where you spend time.

Why do analog clocks make a difference? It's because when we experience the physical clock hands move, *we see time pass,* and we can better perceive how much time we've spent on a particular task. Our brain responds to this differently than a glance at our cell phone. This is why we recommend still using a traditional wristwatch or choosing the analog face setting on your smart watch.

Cell phones can also be useful. An alarm clock app can be a good reminder tool for time-sensitive activities. We recommend setting alarms for recurring tasks—such as when it's time to leave the house for piano lessons, when a medication needs to be taken, or when the mortgage payment is due.

Teaching clients time awareness helps them get out of the house on time to make it to appointments, and it helps them catch themselves when they've spent hours scrolling through social media posts. But time awareness is just one of the many tools needed to accomplish what you need to each day.

Decision Fatigue

As discussed in the Power Shopper chapter, decision fatigue is the concept that each day we have a finite amount of energy to devote to making sound decisions. As the day goes on, our ability to make good decisions wanes. That is why the saying "sleep on it" really works! Every morning, we wake up with new energy to make solid decisions.

You may have heard that certain CEOs wear the same (or a very similar) outfit, day after day. It's true, and they do this, in part, because of decision fatigue. If you are a leader of industry and you must make critical decisions all day, you don't want to waste any decision-making power when you are getting dressed.

Decision fatigue is one of the factors that makes time management so challenging. By the time it's 9:00 p.m. our brains are often fried. Intellectually, we know we *should* go pay bills or plan summer camps, but our ability to choose those tasks over a tantalizing TV show? Gone. It's not that we are lazy.

It's not that we are unmotivated. The reason is that, literally, our ability to make good decisions has been exhausted for the day.

To accomplish what we need to get done, we need to play to our strengths and tackle our task list when our brain is fresh. You might be thinking, "How can I work on my personal to-do list when I am at work all day?" Some people devote time over their lunch hour because they know once they get home at night, it won't happen. Others choose to close out their day by making a list of what they need to do the next day. If the list is done the night before, it's in our subconscious, and we feel more focused when we wake up.

Another way to minimize decision fatigue is to simplify the day as much as possible. Make fewer decisions in total, all day, saving decision-making energy for later when you are tired after a long day. This may be the time when you need all the brain power at your disposal—to force yourself to take care of home management tasks, instead of turning on Netflix!

If you would like to make fewer decisions every day, consider trying some of these simple changes to your routine:

- Eat the same breakfast every morning and drive the same route to work.
- Simplify your wardrobe down to a small number of coordinating pieces. It is the capsule wardrobe concept. To save time and decision-making power, some people choose to wear jeans and a black top most days. Another strategy is to photograph your favorite outfits, hang the clothes together, and viola—no decisions needed.
- Do your hair and make-up the same way every day.
- Always keep your keys and coat in the same exact place.
- Use the same purse every day. Keep the purse in the same spot.
- Check your email only at a few specific pre-selected times during the day. Do the same with social media. Consider using the Time Timer visual timer next to your computer monitor to monitor social media viewing. This timer allows you to see time moving.
- Use the same meal plan for each week. We like to schedule Taco Tuesdays and Pizza Fridays!

- Pick a brand of product you like and stick with it. That way, when shopping, you won't waste your decision-making ability on which yogurt to choose.
- Try the app FocusAtWill.com. It creates soothing background music that also cues time limits. Play a soothing playlist while online shopping and stop when the time is up.

Reducing your choices decreases the number of decisions you make during the day. This will leave you with more ability to make sound decisions later, allowing you to cross more items off that long to-do list.

Finally, to preserve our decision-making power, sometimes we can limit ourselves to only doing one thing at a time. Multitasking—doing multiple activities at once—has been a popular productivity strategy. But, it turns out that our brains are just quickly switching back-and-forth between activities—not completing tasks simultaneously.

We are not actually being more effective while multitasking. So, when you think you should check email while you brush your teeth, you are just asking your brain to work extra hard. Eliminate that second activity. Let brushing your teeth simply be about enjoying good dental hygiene!

Just being aware of decision fatigue helps us make better decisions. But, tackling your to-do list early in the day, simplifying your day, and eliminating unnecessary decisions can result in increased productivity and improved decision-making all day long.

Impulsivity

We all act impulsively at one time or another. And that's not all bad! After all, the word *impulsive* can also mean *spontaneous*. Being too rigid or never trying anything new would make us very boring humans indeed. On the other hand, frequently changing directions can mean we wander through our day chasing shiny things, getting nothing accomplished, and wondering what happened.

ADHD, anxiety, depression, and sleep deprivation can all increase impulsivity. It is helpful to note some of the key symptoms of impulsivity:

- Acting on a whim with little or no forethought even though the action may result in undesirable consequences.
- Taking part in unplanned activities.
- Doing the first thing that pops into your head, rather than what's on the to-do list.
- Choosing short-term gains over long-term outcomes.

Taking off on an expensive weekend trip when money is tight or signing up for a time-consuming event in the middle of a busy time are a couple examples of impulsivity. The key is to slow down, become aware of your feelings, and evaluate your choices—keep your goals in sight!

Create visual reminders of your short and long-term goals and post them somewhere where you'll see them—a whiteboard works nicely.

Keeping your goals in mind doesn't mean you can't have fun! For instance, say you decide to go to the park with your kids. If you spend three hours there, you might begin to worry that your to-do list won't get done. But, you could also decide to set a time limit on the park visit and leave time to complete your to-do list for that day also.

Before jumping into any activity, ask yourself a few questions:

- What are my goals for today?
- What else should I be doing right now?
- What tasks do I need to complete today?

Time management is an oxymoron. Time is beyond our control, and the clock keeps ticking regardless of how we lead our lives. Priority management is the answer to maximizing the time we have.

-John C. Maxwell

Make a Plan

One way to ward off distractions and impulsive tendencies is to write out a plan. Time management experts recommend that we devote one hour on a Sunday afternoon to map out the coming week.

It's ironic, isn't it? In order to be efficient with limited time available, we must dedicate time to planning our time? Yup, that's the skinny. One hour of planning can create three hours of free time in your week.

If organization is not your strong suit, then there is a good chance that attempting to create a plan for your very limited time may not go so well. We have weekly calls with some clients that include creating custom plans and actionable to-do lists.

The plans vary by family, but they might include:

- Writing down (for each member of the family) who needs to be where, at what time, and who is driving them (exhale now).
- The meal plan for every day, whether you are cooking or getting take-out. Who will be cooking? Who is picking up the take-out?
- What groceries or household items need to be bought. We like shared grocery lists, such as those available through an app like Wunderlist. All family members can add items to the grocery list and whoever is shopping can check them off the list too.
- A list of appointments scheduled, and, if they're for a child, who is taking them.
- Errands that need to be attended to and who is responsible.
- Who is taking care of the mail and the bills.
- Phone calls that need to be made, and who is responsible.

A super organized woman we know writes a detailed timeline for the next day in a notebook. She does this right before going to bed each night. She says it actually helps her sleep better, knowing there's a schedule of everything that needs to happen.

She works full time and her husband works from home, so he has some flexibility to help with the after-school activities. She says this daily list keeps them both sane. For her, the process of getting everything out of her head and down on paper eases her anxiety that something might be missed. It helps her communicate with her husband and children. For her husband, the daily list lets him plan his workday. The list saves them a lot of texting back and forth.

A Sample Notebook Entry

2:40 p.m. Anna home on bus (ask her about her history test)

2:50 p.m. Colin home on bus (football practice today)

Mom home at 6:30 p.m. (meetings in Seattle until 5 p.m.)

3:30 p.m. Dad help Colin with physical therapy stretches (straps in laundry room in black bin)

3:45 p.m. Colin ice your knees (wrap a dish towel around the ice pack; set timer for 10 minutes)

4:00 p.m. Colin dressed for football

4:15 p.m. Dad drive Colin to football practice

Dad pick up groceries on the way back from dropping off Colin

  -veggies for salad

  -1% milk

  -breakfast sausage

  -cat food

> **4:30 - 5:00 p.m.** Anna dog walking, homework
>
> *Mark start dinner*
>
> Mom pick up Colin after football practice, home 6:30ish
>
> **7:00 p.m.** Dinner
>
> **7:30 p.m.** Colin homework, physical therapy stretches, and ice knees
>
> **7:45 p.m.** Anna dance class – Mom drives
>
> **9:00 p.m.** Anna gets ride home with Linda

All clients might benefit from creating a list that resembles this one. Having a scheduled call with us not only helps them create the list, but also provides accountability for executing the tasks listed. The idea is that they are more likely to make a phone call they've been dreading, because they know we will ask about it in our call.

To-Do List

We all have to-do lists. Sticky notes with a quick scribbled reminder. Journals with long lists of goals. Are your lists helping manage your time? Often, they are not.

Growing up, not all of us were taught how to make a to-do list, and using these lists effectively doesn't come naturally to many of us. Knowing how to create and use a to-do list is one of the best ways we can remain productive amid the onslaught of all that is being asked of us. A good to-do list can make you feel in control. A good to-do list can help you be productive.

There are many ways to put together a to-do list, but it's best to keep things simple:

- Before you go to bed, write down five things you need to get done the next day. Keep a pen and small pad of paper or some sticky notes on your nightstand. The key is to do this EVERY NIGHT.
- If you prefer, enter the to-do list into a productivity app, like Wunderlist or Evernote.
- Keep the list with you always. Create the same list on your phone, put the paper in your purse, or keep it on the kitchen counter. The idea is that the list is visible to you at all times.
- Any to-dos that don't get done, go on the list for tomorrow. If a task stays on the list for three days, then, on the fourth day, it should be at the top of the list and get done first.
- If you notice that you consistently do not get the five items done, then make the list three items long, and start there.

Break It Down

When an item on our to-do list is daunting, we may be less likely to ever get to it. Sometimes, it is helpful to write out all the steps—down to the micro level—and attack the task one tiny step at a time. Completing one small portion each day can help build momentum. Let's say, for example, that you want to create a baby photo book. Completing the entire project in one day (or even one week) seems unrealistic.

Consider the following sample breakdown of tasks:

Sample Task Breakdown

Complete one step each day:

- Create a file folder on your computer for the baby book project.
- Download photos from your phone to baby book folder.

- Devote one half an hour each day (set a timer on your phone or use a Time Timer visual timer) to download photos until you have a good selection for your baby book. This step may take several days.
- Edit your selected photos, deleting blurry or duplicate pictures.
- Upload photos to the website where you will create your photo book.
- Organize and put photos in the order you prefer. You may need to do this step over several days.
- Finalize your photo album.
- Order your baby book.

This is only an example. Depending on the project you are working on, your breakdown may require more steps. If you find yourself not moving forward with your project even after breaking it down, that may be a signal that you need outside help—even if it's only to have someone check in with you on your progress.

Client Scenario Resolutions

Alicia's Troublesome Tasks

For Alicia, completing necessary household tasks was always reactive instead of proactive. She shopped for groceries at the last minute and didn't plan for meals. Hence, she was invariably missing needed ingredients when cooking dinner. To help her, we systematized online grocery shopping and strategized meal planning. We created a simple weekly meal plan and an associated grocery list.

In the past, she and Adam shared bill paying duties, but didn't always know what the other had taken care of or what bills were still outstanding. We helped Alicia and Adam institute a family meeting every Sunday to plan the week's calendar and to-do list.

We added admin time to their week when they paid bills together after Nathan was asleep. In addition, the couple decided to engage in time management coaching with us every two weeks. They have met with a financial advisor, and now have a clear idea of their finances and how they can achieve their goal of buying a home.

To resolve the complex insurance bill situation, Adam and Alicia took part of a vacation day when they had childcare to make phone calls and resolve issues. Once they got all the bills under control, they rewarded themselves by doing a fun activity together—just the two of them.

Alicia worked with a professional organizer over several weekends to organize her extensive hair care product collection. Now, she has large labeled totes with various products and has a good idea of her inventory.

Cindy's Anxious Mornings

What happened to our clients Cindy and Todd? We worked with Cindy, Amanda, and Chloe to downsize clothing and accessories. During these sessions, the girls completed several loads of laundry in an effort to find the floor of their room. We worked with them to assess what clothes they had and wanted to keep, and which they no longer needed. We decluttered to create storage space.

We estimated that we reduced the overall volume of clothes (and therefore laundry) by 25 percent. The girls were surprised at how many of the clothes no longer fit. We created a checklist of easy chores the older girls could help with in the evening, such as emptying the dishwasher, reading to Samantha, and putting away laundry.

We also designed a morning checklist for the girls, fostering independence. This allowed Cindy to focus on the preschooler, Samantha. We made a detailed timeline for the morning to help the family get out of the house and get everyone to school on time, including Samantha! We utilized phone app alarms as cues to help keep track of time. And, we installed an analog clock in the bathroom as a visual cue to help keep the family on schedule.

Cindy and Todd agreed to spend time each Sunday planning for the upcoming week and noting special activities or appointments. Todd has taken on planning the kids' summer camps—something he had time to research and book during the work week.

Finally, we worked with Cindy to decrease the family's volume of mail by unsubscribing them from catalogs (CatalogChoice.org) and junk mailings (OptOutPreScreen.com). Cindy has asked the nanny to bring in the mail when she brings Samantha home from preschool every day. The mail is now placed in a "hot box", a standing file folder box on the kitchen counter, where Cindy can process through it each night.

We meet with Cindy every two months to catch up on filing and decluttering. Cindy's weeks are still challenging, but the household is running more smoothly, and she is more confident that fewer important tasks and events are falling through the cracks.

Recap – Strategies for The Easily Distracted

Our busy days require that we function optimally, but we are only human. Sometimes, we just aren't as productive as we need to be. By taking small steps toward better time management and implementing one idea at a time, you'll likely notice the positive impact. Get time management coaching to help you plan and stay on track. Remember, getting in shape is easier when you have the support of a trainer.

Here is a recap of the main topics and strategies covered in this chapter that will help you gain control of your schedule.

Easily Distracted Strategies	**Strategy Details**
Improve your productivity.	• Turn off distractions that you can control. • Improve your time awareness by using analog clocks and alarms. • Simplify your daily routine to preserve decision-making capabilities. • Ward off impulses with visual cues of your short and long-term goals and boundaries.
Use tools that work for you.	• Write out and follow a detailed daily plan. • Make a simple to-do list each day. • Breakdown complex tasks into micro tasks.

Notes

What ideas spoke to you?

_____
_____
_____
_____

In the Words of Our Clients

I have worked with Amy Nelson of Simplify Experts ever since meeting her at an ADHD conference over six years ago. I was a single mom desperate to help my 12-year-old son who had just been diagnosed with ADD, and also gain some coping skills for myself. We were both chronically disorganized, and I was afraid my home disorganization was contributing to his school disorganization.

Amy, quite frankly, changed our LIVES. She was so understanding and compassionate. She cut right through the issues, while still listening to our reasoning, our fears, and our challenges. We were VERY organized by the time she was done with us—in just one day. EVERYTHING had a place, and she hauled away everything we didn't need.

I have used her several times since then, as our family's needs have changed. I got married, blending families together so our space changed.

Amy and her team have been SO FANTASTIC. She is almost like part of our family now. She knows each family member and knows their challenges. Simplify Experts is a team that truly specializes in listening to what you need. They identify things that aren't working for you and customize solutions for the long term.

Our maintenance appointments and spring cleanings are now practically joyful, I love calling her and her team to come help me find my bliss—a beautifully organized home that works for our current needs.

–Simplify Experts Client

Chapter 7

THE OVERBURDENED EMPLOYEE

Your disorganization at work thwarts your career success. You are working hard, but your performance reviews are worse each year. Your nerves are shot. It's hard to focus with coworkers dropping by. The emails keep coming in, and it's hard to stay on task. You often work late to catch up or meet deadlines. It has become hard to disengage from work. Being disorganized at work is taking a toll on your whole life. You experience constant pressure. You are disorganized both at work and at home.

Client Scenarios

Beverly's Work Files

Beverly works for the government. She feels constantly stressed and overwhelmed at work. To cope, she shops. She showed me three rooms, each full of clothing. She is sleeping in the guest bedroom because her own bed is buried in clothes.

At home, Beverly has a hard time staying in any of these rooms for more than 15 minutes; the clutter is overwhelming and makes her anxious. Beverly said that although she and her husband would like to entertain, they have not had anyone to their home for over a year.

While we discussed organizing her home, Beverly mentioned that at work, her desk and files were a big source of stress. Her job entails updating several documents each month. Accuracy is critical.

Beverly said that she struggles to remember where she saved the documents on her computer. She recently spent days recreating documents she was unable to locate. As a result, she had to spend many extra hours at work trying to catch up.

Beverly has an employee review coming up, and she is terrified that her job might be in danger. Her last two reviews indicated that she needs to improve her time management and the quality of her work. She called us as a last resort, not knowing who else to turn to.

Tina's Promotion

Tina called us to schedule an organizing appointment after she was told she needed to clean up her desk space at work. She is a software engineer who works for a large tech company in the Seattle area. She has been in her current role for several years and is due for a promotion. While her overall track record is solid, Tina is concerned about one area where she has struggled her entire life—meeting deadlines.

When Tina and I met in her home, she described how in college she'd stay up all night to get assignments completed, turning them in at the last minute. She secured extensions from professors when she could. Now that she is an adult, she has a harder time staying up all night before a deadline. She doesn't sleep well. She's often up until 2:00 a.m. or later, but it's not productive time.

Waking up and getting to work, is a bleary struggle. She usually arrives by 10:00 a.m. and works until 7:00 p.m. or later. At work, she subsists on coffee and energy drinks. Her desk is a jumble of papers and empty energy drink cans. When a deadline is looming, she gets into what she calls "the zone" at around 7:00 p.m. and works late to complete her project—just in time.

Factors Impacting Disorganization at Work

Clients often tell us that they are organized at work, but not at home. Or, just the opposite, they say they are not organized at work, but their home is tidy. When both work and home are disorganized, it's a crisis for many individuals.

> **Tired minds don't plan well. Sleep first, plan later.**
> – Walter Reisch

Disorganized at Home, Disorganized at Work

Work and home are interrelated in many ways. Your home supports your ability to get to work on time and impacts your productivity. While an organized house is important, a peaceful bedroom is essential. If you are not getting quality sleep, it's more challenging to get to work on time and to be productive while you are there.

We build large master bedroom suites with the intention of using them as an oasis for rest and relaxation. Then, we turn our master bedroom into a playroom, an office, or home theater, all of which can sabotage good sleep—and, as a result, undermine productivity at work.

Quality rest fosters productivity. We need about eight hours of sleep, but an estimated 41 million people (30 percent of American workers), don't get the rest they need to be productive, according to the Centers for Disease Control and Prevention[6].

---

[6] Weber, Lauren. "Go Ahead, Hit the Snooze Button." *Wall Street Journal.* 23 January 2013. Web. Jan. 2018.

So, how can we improve our sleep? For starters, leave the electronics out of your bedroom. Watching TV in the bedroom disrupts the quality and quantity of our sleep. At night, charge your cell phone in a room other than the bedroom. Don't use your cell phone as an alarm clock.

Cluttered surfaces in our bedrooms cause visual overstimulation. When we are trying to get a good night's sleep, we usually have enough on our minds without being distracted by paperwork piles, unread books, toys, and anything else cluttering the bedroom. Paperwork is a to-do item that belongs in the office or on your desk. Unread books should reside on a bookshelf.

If your children play in your bedroom, make it a point to return their toys to their rooms each night. Your bedroom is an adult space where you shouldn't have to walk through a sea of LEGO™ pieces or stuffed animals on your way to the closet. Remove everything that doesn't belong in your bedroom.

When we haven't slept enough and have cluttered closets, it's no wonder we struggle getting to work on time. It takes time to wade through all those clothes, especially if you are groggy. One trick is to simplify how you get dressed and even what you wear to work. Choosing what to wear when one has a small, capsule wardrobe is much easier than selecting from hundreds of outfit options. If we can't find our shoes, it slows down our morning routine. When we store our shoes in a dedicated shoe rack, we are more likely to get to work on time. Makes sense, right?

> **Think in the morning. Act in the noon.
> Eat in the evening. Sleep in the night.**
>
> - WILLIAM BLAKE

Workplace Distractions

When you struggle to stay organized and productive at work, external distractions are often the culprit. You might be distracted by coworkers dropping by or talking loudly on phones. Personal emails or texts present other distractions.

A computer constantly pinging with new messages and notifications creates enough tiny interruptions to break your concentration. Many of the emails we receive don't require our immediate attention, but the notifications are enough to break our focus. According to a *Fast Company* article about task switching, it takes people about 23 minutes to fully refocus on work[7].

You may not be able to eliminate every distraction, but you can decrease them. Here are some examples of things you can try:

- Keep your phone on silent in a drawer and check it only at set times.
- Reduce email distractions by unsubscribing from unnecessary email lists.
- Close your email program completely and choose specific times during the day to check email. Alternatively, if your job requires you to check and send email frequently, change software preferences to download inbound email at set times.
- If you can't remove the distraction, remove yourself when you need a period of uninterrupted work time (working, for example in an empty conference room).

Therapy for Your Workspace

Like it or not, cluttered, disorganized workspaces can alter how coworkers perceive us. Recently, a friend of mine lamented that she couldn't find a specific hard copy of a form at work—something that she uses almost daily.

As it turns out, over the last few years, a lot of her workspace has been overtaken by boxes of pamphlets sent by various vendors. Over time, the boxes have just piled up and slowly taken over her workspace. One day, this clutter swallowed up the form she needed, creating a lot of unneeded stress. When desk clutter goes unchecked, it impacts your ability to do your job effectively.

---

[7] Pattison, Kermit. "Worker, Interrupted: The Cost of Task Switching." *Fast Company*. 28 June 2008. Web. Jan. 2018.

Set up your workspace so that your most important items are easily visible—front and center. Infrequently used pamphlets, for example, shouldn't share the same desk space as daily used forms. An uncluttered, clean desk at work has countless benefits. A tidy desk calms your mind.

Both your motivation and productivity are likely to increase when your workspace is organized.

- Instead of piles on your desk, store documents in labeled files, either in a drawer or on your desk. Documents will be easily retrievable and will not create visual or physical clutter.
- Remove any items from your desk that are outdated or distracting.
- Consider posting checklists. Some people find it helpful to have a written checklist that details priorities for the week and reminds them of recurring responsibilities.
- Use visual aids, like white boards and mind maps, to outline all the relevant components of a project.
- Appropriate lighting is key to productivity. In some circumstances, a dark room with task lighting can help block out distractions from your surroundings.

Clear the Desk

In addition to clutter, items related to other work projects can distract from a task that needs complete focus. Sometimes, the only remedy is to remove everything from the desk except the very few items related to the specific task at hand. Store other work items behind you, for example, or in another location altogether.

This strategy can also help when working at home. To achieve full focus, clear your desk of personal to-do lists, household bills or statements, and any other items that are not related to the task.

Reaffirm Your Task Focus

Some individuals find it useful to constantly remind themselves, even out loud, "This is what I am working on right now and nothing else."

You may ask yourself, "What is the biggest priority this morning? What is the biggest priority today?" Visualize your day and think specifically about the tasks you will be working on.

Focus on completing small parts of the task. Imagine how you will feel when you complete the entire task. This running narrative will keep your mind on the task and away from distractions.

Prioritizing Tasks

It's tough to be productive when you don't know where to start. You may have a long list in front of you, but you are unsure of the priorities. It's never a bad idea to get clarification on priorities from your boss: "You've asked me to do these 10 things, what are the top three priorities?" Sometimes to stay on top of your job, you may need to say "no" to low-priority or optional commitments.

It's also a good idea to confirm due dates. If you don't have a clear deadline, you may have trouble getting started and planning your days. Sometimes, you may need to set a deadline for yourself and use an accountability partner who will hold you to that deadline (see chapter 8—Clutter Clearing System).

Plan your project work by starting with the final deadline and working backwards to identify smaller, interim deadlines. To keep yourself on track toward the deadline, schedule regular check-ins with your team or manager. If necessary, set up frequent, short meetings with your boss or an accountability partner.

Getting Started

Most of us know whether we are a morning person or a night person. We know when we tend to get the most done, and the time of day when it's easiest to tackle difficult tasks. Maximize your productivity by working on difficult tasks that require focus during your most productive time of day. Some individuals, for example, go into the office early before anyone else, capitalizing on their ability to work efficiently in the morning and taking advantage of the quiet time to focus on work. Others get more accomplished by staying after hours; the time when their productivity really ramps up.

What if you are not feeling motivated to start? We suggest setting a reward for yourself before you begin. The reward can be anything—even something small—as long as it feels like a reward to you.

Motivation tends to build as we start to work, even if we are only able to complete a tiny task. Action begets action—meaning that just starting and doing any small part of your task will help build momentum. After completing a small part of the task, take a short break, and give yourself a small reward. Think of the long-term benefit of completing the task, then set another small benchmark and another small reward.

In addition to the above rewards and accountability you create for yourself, you can also maintain your motivation by using external accountability—regularly touching base with your manager or accountability partner.

The key is to consistently repeat the cycle over and over again:

1. Set a small reward for completing a small task.
2. Complete task.
3. Enjoy reward.
4. Set next task and reward.
5. Complete task. Repeat step 4, and so on.

We've also learned that working on the same task for an extended period or "sustaining effort" can be very difficult. Some people begin a work project (excitedly even), but then get derailed when they reach a tough point and may be unable to continue. Others begin a project, get bored, and lose momentum.

Individuals who suffer from brain-based conditions, such as ADHD, often find sustaining effort to be especially difficult. In these instances, individuals need to develop specific strategies to help them.

This is tough stuff. Strategies we have used with clients are similar to those used when we need to get motivated to get started. If completing the next task becomes too difficult, use a timer and work on a small part for five minutes (just to overcome the paralysis). The completion of even the smallest, five-minute task can increase motivation to do more. Then, start the timer for another five minutes.

These short, fixed intervals keep people focused on a small, manageable part, rather than the overwhelming entirety of the project. Keep your eye on the prize of completing the task and reaching the next small goal. Share your challenges and achievements with an accountability partner and keep going.

You might also try the widely popular Pomodoro Technique. Set a timer and work for 25 minutes. Take a three to five minute break. Once you've done this four times in a row, take a longer 10 to 15 minute break. During each break, acknowledge your progress or share your progress with someone else. Then, give yourself a small reward and recharge yourself by getting some fresh air.

Procrastination

We all procrastinate. We may delay beginning a task if we have mixed feelings about it or if we think we lack the necessary skills. Sometimes, we spend too much time working on other, less critical tasks before focusing on what's important. This may also include not starting until everything is set up ("I need coffee and a muffin") or until you are in "the right mood."

Becoming aware of specific procrastination habits can help us fight them. In addition to the rewards and short time intervals we discussed earlier, we can avoid procrastination by creating accountability. That means telling another person how and when we will complete specific tasks. If we know someone is going to ask how the task is going, then we are more likely to be on it. Sometimes, this may mean just having the second person in the same room while you are working. Ultimately, we are less likely to procrastinate if someone else is checking up on us.

Work Organization and Career Clarity

Getting organized allows you to see your bigger purpose. We worked with a gentleman who had run his own company for years. He knew he wasn't good at staying organized. We organized all his paperwork and financial documents, which gave him a greater sense of control over the current state of his business. He had a better idea of what might be possible in the future. The work we completed opened up his eyes to bigger opportunities; he used the work we did as a springboard and sold his business later that year.

For another client, getting organized at work lead to the realization that their job wasn't a good fit. They had attributed their unhappiness at work to disorganization, but, once that barrier was removed, they realized that the job itself wasn't right and started looking for new opportunities.

Client Scenario Resolutions

Beverly's Work Files

We met Beverly at her office with two goals in mind. We wanted to make sure she would always be able to find the files she needed on her computer. We also wanted to create a hard copy checklist of what needed to be done for each file.

First, we decluttered Beverly's computer desktop, deleting unneeded files. Then, we created clearly labeled folder shortcuts on the computer desktop, so Beverly could easily find the files she needed. We talked about the company's file storage system, and Beverly learned how to name files on the network and how to create shortcuts on the computer desktop. We documented file locations, and how to save and find files. We created step-by-step checklists for each recurring task, and posted those checklists in clear view from Beverly's chair.

We decluttered her desk and work files. She loved her tidy workspace and felt empowered to complete her work. A few weeks later, Beverly called to tell us how relieved she felt; work had been going better for her.

She wanted to continue working with us at her home. We met on a Saturday morning, and we could tell right away that Beverly was feeling very anxious. We talked about her goals for her home. Beverly wanted to be able to sleep in her own bedroom with her husband. To achieve this goal, we had to address the clothing piles on and around her bed. We could tell this task felt overwhelming to Beverly; she had difficulty staying in the bedroom.

So, instead, we brought the work to the living room by filling up a laundry basket with clothes from the bedroom and sorting them in the living room. We made three piles: laundry, clothes to hang up, and clothes to donate. Slowly, basket after basket, we cleared the space on the bed and floor.

Once Beverly was able to use her own bedroom, we created a wardrobe inventory card (see the Power Shopper chapter). When Beverly shopped, she referred to this card and was able to make better buying decisions. Whenever Beverly began to feel overwhelmed at work, we scheduled a call and strategized solutions.

Tina's Promotion

When Tina described her situation, we knew right away that she would benefit from an improved sleep schedule. She mentioned that if she can't sleep at night, she watches TV and plays video games. As a result, Tina's bedroom looked more like a media room than a place to sleep. Since Tina has had insomnia for as long she can remember, she never thought that TV and video games in her bedroom could be making it worse.

Tina decided to move the TV and gaming console to another room. Then, we wrote down a list of ideas to help her fall asleep earlier. She decided to make an appointment with a sleep specialist to find out what could be causing her insomnia.

We worked on simplifying Tina's morning routine so that she would be able to arrive at work by 9:00 a.m. We organized both her closet and her bathroom. In her closet, we separated work clothes from casual clothes. We moved Tina's shoes and organized them on a shoe rack.

In the bathroom, we downsized products and put everyday toiletries into one bin, making it easy for her to get ready in the morning. We added two clocks—one in her bathroom and one in her closet—to help create time awareness during the morning. We created a smoothie station in her kitchen so that Tina can make breakfast and get out the door quickly. Finally, we set a phone alarm to remind Tina when it was time to leave.

Tina asked her manager if she could work with us at her office over the weekend. To help Tina get her work done without having to stay late, we worked to reduce distractions in her workspace. We cleared the desk, placing items not related to the highest priority project behind her. Tina identified a small conference room on another floor of her building where she could go and work if her current workstation was too distracting.

Recap – Strategies for the Overburdened Employee

When we feel disorganized at home and at work, then every part of our day feels overwhelming. Being organized at home results in better focus and performance at work. Being organized at work results in a less stressful workday.

The following tips may get you started, but if you struggle both at work and home, it's time to get help.

Overburdened Employee Strategies	Strategy Details
Reduce distractions.	• Keep your phone on silent in a drawer. • Unsubscribe from unnecessary email lists. • Check email at set times. • Change email software preferences to download inbound email at set times. • Remove yourself to a quieter space.
Create your workspace.	• Remove piles from desk. • File work documents. • Post task checklists. • Use whiteboards to outline tasks.
Clear the desk to focus.	• Remove everything from your desk that isn't critical for your current task.
Reaffirm task focus.	• State your focus repeatedly to yourself and others.

Identify top priorities and establish deadlines.	• Clarify top priorities with manager. • Set deadlines for intermediary steps in a project. • Schedule check-ins with manager.
Set rewards for getting started.	• Identify most productive time of day. • Set a small reward for completing a small task, work to complete the task, enjoy your reward, repeat. • Check in with manager or accountability partner.
Improve ability to sustain effort.	• Break paralysis by using timer and working in 5-minute increments; acknowledge progress, repeat. Use rewards to keep going. • Use the Pomodoro Technique.
Battle procrastination.	• Identify how you procrastinate. • Proclaim your goal to another person for accountability. • Use a buddy/body double to work alongside you, keeping you on track.

Notes

What ideas spoke to you?

_____

_____

_____

_____

In the Words of Our Clients

Imagine how thrilled I was the morning my director walked to my orderly desk and asked for something. In less than five seconds, I was able to reach in my file drawer, find the file, and hand her what she needed. I smiled on and off all day.

Something as simple as that would have previously required a search through three or more piles (depending on the week) and a promise to get it to her within the hour.

A lot of stress is gone in my life as a result of your help. Thank you very much!

Now, will you come over and help me with "Quick...whatever-it's-called"? I'm ready to get my finances on track again.

–Simplify Experts Client

Chapter 8

THE CLUTTER CLEARING SYSTEM

Ready to start decluttering? Nervous? Skeptical? It's completely understandable—after all, you've tried to get organized before and didn't have success.

But, you can leave your worries behind! With the right strategies and the right help, you can and will have an organized life. We've spent a lot of time discussing why so many of us struggle with disorganization. Now, it is time to take that awareness and move toward engagement. It's time for your home or office to get a fresh start.

Accountability Partner

To reiterate, you do *not* need to do this alone. In fact, if you've failed at getting organized in the past, we strongly urge you *not* to work on organizing alone. Why? You will be so much more successful working with an accountability partner.

Don't get stuck on that hamster wheel again. Hard work is easier when done with a partner. To help you organize, recruit someone to help. Perhaps a friend or family member—someone to stay by your side as you work, be your buddy/body double and accountability partner.

The following is a description of what an accountability partner should be:

- A cheerleader – like a health coach or a life coach, not there to judge or shame, but rather to encourage, inspire, and support.
- A motivator – providing external accountability.
- An extra set of ears – listening to your needs and goals.
- A patient, steadfast partner – someone who will stick with you for the duration.
- An objective partner – someone who is invested in helping you succeed.

The Benefits of a Professional Organizer

In many cases, a friend or family member doesn't quite meet the criteria of what you need from an accountability partner. A friend you typically have over for a chat and a glass of wine is probably not interested in helping you declutter your garage or bathroom. Friends may not have the patience to go through endless piles of paperwork with you. Admittedly, it is a big ask.

Family members might be willing to help you tackle a garage, but going through heirlooms may bring out their own emotions—which may not be in line with yours.

Working with a professional organizer vastly improves your chances of conquering existing clutter. In addition to meeting the criteria of a great accountability partner, professional organizers bring the following skills:

- **Focus.** An organizer focuses completely on your needs and on the task at hand.
- **Supplies.** A professional organizer arrives with all the supplies and products needed for organizing. There is no need to find your label maker, manila folders, or even trash bags.
- **Product Knowledge.** Professional organizers bring an understanding of what organizing products work and which products are best suited for specific spaces. There is no need for you to shop for orga-

nizing products, wondering whether you are purchasing the correct items.
- **Paperwork Expertise.** Professional organizers know the ins-and-outs of which documents you need to keep, how long, and why.
- **Efficiency.** The amount of work achieved in a three-hour session with an organizer will take 10-plus hours working on your own. Who has that kind of time these days? Not many of us. Three hours is much more efficient.
- **Passion.** Organizers love to organize! They know how to make every corner of your home and office efficient, and how to simplify processes. Mostly, organizers want to help you live your best life.

The value of a strong accountability partner is well reflected in the following comments provided by one of our clients.

> *Working with Denise and her team was a delight. Every step of the way, there were well-planned strategies tailored to my needs. In a clear, supportive way, she was able to teach me how to maintain the new organization systems that we set up.*
>
> *As a smart consumer it really was worth every penny. She works hard to get the most done in the least amount of time. Her expert guidance and patient support created the conditions for my greater success professionally and personally.*
>
> *After reading all the books on organization without luck, I thought I was doomed to live with a cluttered office. Denise helped me build and sustain organization routines for my teaching materials and work space.*
>
> –Simplify Experts Client

So, what is the secret sauce our professional organizers use to tackle clutter and create an organized space? We use our Clutter Clearing System methodology.

In short, the steps include:

- Identifying a vision for the space to be organized.
- Instructions on how to sort your items, including tricky items such as heirlooms.
- A method for assigning items a specific location or home.
- Strategies for labeling and containing items.
- Tools for maintaining an organized home or work office.

Step 1: Form a Vision for the Space

Grab a notepad and walk around each room of your home. In each room, ask yourself—what are the activities that occur in this space? Then, ask yourself, what activities *should* take place in this room? Do you use your dining room to entertain friends and family? If not, perhaps that dining room can be repurposed as your craft room or sewing space. Or perhaps it's the other way around—you've been using your dining room for crafts, but you want to entertain and eat meals at the dining room table.

Next, take note of what *doesn't* belong in each space. Do you have golf clubs in your living room? Do you have piles of paper on the counter in the kitchen (where you could be prepping food)? Are there toys in your bathroom? Are there boxes in the hallway? What does not belong in your office?

Finally, for each room, imagine how you would like the space to feel. For example, would you like the space to feel open and calm? Would you like the space to feel like the family hub? Are you not using a particular room for its intended purpose?

As you write it all down, you're taking the first, important step towards creating a better, more organized life.

Use the same tactic if your goal is to organize your workplace environment. Scan your workplace from left to right, and write down what doesn't belong in the space. What distracts you? Imagine what a productivity inducing space might look and feel like to you. We perform this exercise with our clients during our initial meeting. Then, we devise a plan of attack.

Step 2: Sort and Let Go

A cluttered room can look overwhelming. All you see is stuff, and it's unclear where to start. It's less intimidating to start sorting items on one side of the room and make your way to the other. Often, we start on the left side of a room and move toward the right.

If the space is very cluttered, it can be helpful to put down tape to divide the space or even throw a sheet over the clutter to mark a smaller area of focus. This keeps the focus of sorting items in a clearly defined space. We always take a "before" photo so you can watch your progress!

As you sort items, decide what category it belongs in:

- **Items to keep.** These are items you love, utilize, or reference.
- **Items to donate.** Items you are no longer using, don't need, don't like, or, for whatever reason, they don't work for you. Put donations in black trash bags or cardboard boxes. Cardboard boxes are good for books (they get heavy). Fragile items should also be put into boxes to ensure they arrive at the donation center in one piece. If you'd like a record for tax purposes, use a clipboard and write down all items you are donating. To check the value of items you are donating, use the valuation guide at Goodwill's website (Goodwill.org). It's not necessary to log each individual item. You may just note down general information such as: one large table, six pairs of jeans, two coats, etc.
- **Trash.** Use white kitchen trash bags. By using black bags for donations and white for garbage, it's easier to keep clear what's going where.
- **Recycling.** Let's get the recycling out to your recycle bin. With black and white bags already filling roles, we like using tall paper leaf bags (found at hardware stores) for recycling. In most locations, you can set them next to your recycle bin at the curb and they'll be taken away on trash day at no cost.
- **Shredding.** Anything with your name, address, phone number, social security number, or bank account number should be shredded.

If you are not sure whether a document should be shredded, consult the Federal Trade Commission website (Consumer.ftc.gov).

- **Items that belong in another room.** Keep these items just outside the room's threshold. Once you are done in this space, your homework is to deliver these items to where they belong.
- **Items missing a part.** These are items you are unable to use or donate because they are missing parts. Keep a box of these items while you declutter in case you find the missing part as you work. Anything left over at the end is trash.

Work through the space using these guidelines. Does it seem daunting? We schedule three-hour sessions with our clients because we've noticed that most people can't work any longer than that. Sorting involves making a lot of decisions—and that's mentally taxing. If you have worked for two hours and you notice that you are feeling tired, take out the recycling and trash, drive your donations to a donation center, and call it a day. Continue working on the space the next time you are able. As you sort and make decisions, keep in mind the following two "Golden Rules."

Golden Rules

Rule 1: 80 percent is full. This applies to all cupboards, drawers, and closets. In your closets, you need hangers to have swing space for ease of retrievability. If you find that you are jamming your hangers in, then your closet is too full. It's time to reduce the volume so your closet is *at most* 80 percent full. The same goes for all the storage areas in your house.

The Pareto principle (also known as the 80–20 rule) is the idea that roughly 80 percent of the effects (in any given area) come from 20 percent of the causes. At the organizing level, for example, people tend to wear 20 percent of their clothing 80 percent of the time. Many of us have closets full of items we wear less than once a year (or not at all). The same concept applies in all the other areas of our home. In the bathroom, we use 20 percent of our products 80 percent of the time. In the kitchen, we use 20 percent of our kitchen tools 80 percent of the time, and so forth. Keep this in mind as you consider letting go of various items.

Rule 2: Make decisions only about items that belong to you. You must get permission before sorting items belonging to other family members. Set aside items that belong to others so that they may decide on their own. Yes, you may really hate that ratty T-shirt your husband has been wearing since college, but he's got to be on board before it gets tossed. After all, you would ask the same if the roles were reversed. I make an exception to this rule when organizing young children's toys. As a parent, you know which toys are their favorites and which toys your child hasn't touched in months.

Tough Decisions

As you sort through your belongings and decide what to keep and what to let go, you will certainly come across tricky items. What should you do with gifts you were given, but may not want? What about heirlooms? They may have been in your family for years, but don't really fit your lifestyle. What about memorabilia and keepsakes?

Here is our take on these questions:

The Gift You Received

A wise person once said, the best kind of gift anyone can give you is one that comes with no strings attached. We believe this to be true. If you have thanked the giver warmly, your end of the deal is done. You have no more obligation to that person. You don't need to use, display, or even keep the gift. After all, if you gave someone a gift, would you expect them to keep it their entire lives? Probably not. If you've been given a gift you don't care for, pass that item on to someone who may enjoy it. You get to make decisions about all your things. Gifts are not your children; you <u>do</u> get to choose your favorites.

It's Okay to Say No

What do you give the woman who has everything? It is difficult to buy gifts for Aunt Marilyn. One year at Christmas, someone gave her a small statue of a rhino. She seemed to like the gift, displaying it on her fireplace mantle. Aunt Marilyn is part of a large social circle of women, and many of them noticed that rhino statue. She hosts Bunco games and book club meetings in her home. Since that one fateful Christmas many years ago, she has been gifted more than 90 rhino figurines, paintings, and prints.

We've all seen this happen. If you have a cat or a dog, you may receive cat or dog-related gifts. Aunt Marilyn enjoyed that first rhino gift (although she actually isn't particularly fond of rhinos). Now that her home has been overrun by 90 rhinos, she no longer enjoys her collection. It's okay to communicate that you are over the rhinos (or cats, puppies, or whatever). You might casually say something like:

Do you know what a group of rhinos is called? A "crash." I'm maxed out with my collection. Let's enjoy lunch out together instead of exchanging gifts. It's our time together that I so appreciate.

Well-Intentioned Shoppers

Grandmas are entitled to spoil their grandchildren goes the old saying. Many of us have well-meaning relatives (usually mothers and grandmothers) who love to shop, buying nice things for us and our children. Their intentions are good, even if we may not always agree with their choices.

"Here come the big plastic toys from grandma," you might be thinking. Or, "More fancy clothes my kids will never wear" might be what goes through your mind. Perhaps your daughter is not a fan of dresses, even if grandma bought it at Neiman Marcus.

One client's mom bought entire new wardrobes for her two grandsons before a trip to Hawaii. She bought a different bathing suit and swim top for every day of the vacation as well as new shorts and T-shirts for each. The boys' mother lamented that none of the clothes would fit by next summer.

Clients often ask us how to get these eager gift givers to scale back. We recommend that you delicately convey gratitude to the giver and give them some gift ideas. You might say something like:

We appreciate your thoughtfulness and generosity toward our family; it really speaks to the wonderful person you are.

We are trying to create calm in our home by having fewer belongings. Would it be okay to ask a favor? Would you consider gift options such as a zoo membership, a camp, or children's theater tickets?

Family Heirlooms

We sometimes inherit items that were special to someone else. What if those items don't fit your decor? Your lifestyle? Are you someone who uses silver and fine china? If not, it is okay to let those items go. Choose a small symbolic item that represents the essence of that special family member, but don't feel pressured to keep their entire collection which takes over your storage space.

For example, Denise shared a love of tea and British TV with her grandmother. When her grandmother passed away, she left behind an extensive library of books about the British monarchy and a collection of antique tea sets. These items were very special to her. To honor her memory, Denise chose her white gloves (reminding her of their formal tea afternoons) and one ornate antique tea cup that she has on display. Neither of these items overwhelm her home, and they are the perfect symbol of her relationship with her grandmother.

Memorabilia

When we first have children, each of us believe that their every scribble is proof of their genius. It's hard not to! When our children enter elementary school, we are gifted with daily stacks of their work. As they grow we might save favorite clothes they wore as toddlers. We hang on to special blankets, books, and stuffed animals. Multiply all this by three children and twelve years of school, add in our own memorabilia, and we have a recipe for clutter—extreme edition.

All keepsakes are a reminder of a special time. Maybe you have a bin of T-shirts from every concert you attended over the years. Or perhaps you have all your prom dresses. Perhaps you have a collection of action figures. Keeping in mind that 80 percent of your total available storage space is considered full, how much of that space can you realistically dedicate to memorabilia? Once you determine this allocated space, then that becomes the boundary for your memorabilia collection.

How do we decide what to keep and what to let go? For children's memorabilia, we advise that you don't save anything that looks like busy work—keep only the best sample of their work. Take a photo of items that remind you of a special time in your child's life. One client photographed their child's favorite stuffed animal and a toy truck they really liked, and then they donated these items. For your own memorabilia items, keep those items that are unique or especially meaningful, but consider whether your collection would be a burden for someone else to deal with if something were to happen to you.

Should You Sell it?

Do your research. Items on secondary markets such as Craigslist, eBay, or Offer Up tend to sell for 30 to 40 percent of what a new item would cost. Furniture consignment stores usually require you to email photos, dimensions, and level of wear. If they decide to sell your item, they will charge approximately 50 percent commission. Research, listing, waiting for buyers, it all takes your most valuable commodity – time. A good guideline some of our clients use (for items worth $100 or more on Craigslist) is to try to sell the item for two weeks, and, if it doesn't sell, they donate it.

Wait, I Might Need That One Day!

If you are saving things for just-in-case scenarios, you are not living in the present. Instead, you're thinking about what might (but most likely won't) happen in the future. It's today that counts.

Consider: how easy would it be to replace this item if you needed it in the future? If you can replace an item for roughly $20 in 20 minutes of shopping, then having that item cluttering up your house is not worth it. Let's say you took up knitting a few years back, for example, and after a few months, you put it down and haven't thought about it since. Storing skeins of yarn on the off chance that you take up knitting in the future doesn't make sense.

Wait, I Can Reuse That!

We are the environmentally conscious, recycling, and composting generation. That intention to reuse causes some of us to use precious storage space to house items such as packaging from large electronics—televisions, computers, and the like.

What if I need to return it? What if I need to move? Seemingly reasonable points, but we also need to consider whether storing those boxes is creating a clutter problem in our house. Would that space be better used to store other items, resulting in a calmer, less cluttered home?

Wait, I Spent a Lot on That!

When we spend big on a handbag, shoes, a coat, or a dress, we tend to covet these items more than our day-to-day stuff—they become special. Do you remember your first nice handbag? Long after you had stopped using it, it still held a special spot in your heart—and probably on your closet shelf. It was no longer stylish, but you couldn't make yourself donate it. Your perceived value of this purse was much more than a consignment store would sell it for.

We find that this can be true whether the item was lovingly used or whether it lived in the back a closet with tags still on. When we spend big bucks, we have a harder time saying good-bye—even years later.

Remember, we are not paying for our homes to be a museum of the past. When our available storage for this type of item is over 80 percent full, invoke the *hakuna matata-no worries* philosophy and let the item go.

Gift Closets

Another tricky area to sort is the "gift closet"—an area in the house where new items are stashed with the intention of them being gifts at some point. Gift closets often contribute to clutter and frequently overflow, sometimes taking over entire rooms.

When a gift-giving occasion finally arises, invariably these presents are no longer suitable, and new gifts are purchased. A gift closet often devolves into your own personal version of the Island of Misfit Toys.

When did you give up your home to be a store? Follow these rules to contain the gift area:

- Dedicate one shelf for gifts and stick to that boundary.
- Donate outdated gifts.
- Make a list of gift items.
- Don't buy gifts for the distant future (people change).

Step 3: Assign a Home

Now that you've sorted, the next step in the Clutter Clearing System is to find homes for all the items you are keeping.

Zoning. We recommend you store like items together in one location. For example, keep all the soccer equipment together in one area of the garage or keep all sewing supplies in one closet. You may need to swap storage locations for certain items depending on the season. Camping equipment gets prime storage in summer, for example, while ski equipment takes its place during the winter.

Usage frequency. How often are you accessing this item? Weekly? Monthly? Twice a year? We recommend that you use your prime storage real estate for your frequently used items.

Shelving. Use industrial post shelving to hold bins in your garage or basement. These shelving units come in a variety of sizes and are available at all hardware and organizing stores. Shelving provides better accessibility, (you can compromise your back health if you are frequently stacking heavy bins). Shelves also keep bins safely off the floor.

Lifestyle fit. We recommend to clients that they store items so that their location fits their lifestyle. Holiday platters, for example, can go into holiday bins if they are taking up precious space in your kitchen. But, if you use them regularly throughout the year, then they need to be kept handy in the kitchen. If you are bringing in fresh flowers every week, you need your vases handy. If flowers aren't a regular part of your life, then vases don't need a prime storage location (perhaps they should be kept in the laundry room).

Step 4: Contain and Label

Most people don't realize it, but they go about organizing the wrong way. They start the process by buying containers. Often, these containers don't fit the space where they are needed.

Buying containers is actually the fourth step in the Clutter Clearing System. Here's how to make sure you choose the right container for the right place.

- Grab a measuring tape and write down the width, depth, and height of your storage space. Now, you are ready to shop for containers.
- Drawer organizers keep our personal items from sliding around and keep like items together.
- We recommend clear containers. They give us a quick view of what's inside.
- Opaque containers are fine for annual use items, such as Christmas and Halloween decorations or camping gear.
- When storing personal care products on shelves, you may want to store the containers without the lid, so you can reach in and grab what you need. Use shelf risers so you don't have to stack bins. (Think first aid or nail polish)
- We label small containers clearly with white label tape. We use upper and lowercase lettering because the brain processes upper and lowercase letters faster than all capitals. In the garage or basement, we use a half of a sheet of yellow card stock to label cardboard boxes or opaque bins in large print.

When placing items into bins, consider how much space you want to dedicate to storing back stock. When it comes to personal care products, for example, do you have the space to house an extra eight tubes of toothpaste, ten bottles of shampoo, and twenty lotions? Perhaps having one or two extras of each is plenty. Most of us have frequent access to stores, and we live in a 24/7 society where we can have almost anything delivered to our doorstep.

Step 5: Evaluate and Maintain

Congratulations! Now that your items are sorted and placed in labeled bins, you have completed organizing your space. Have you taken an "after" photo of the space you've organized? Have you revisited your "before" photo?

You have made incredible progress! Whether you organize alone or with a professional organizer, your organized space will be 40 percent easier to maintain. We believe the key is using our Clutter Clearing System.

As time goes by, evaluate if the location where you placed the items still works for you. If not, make adjustments. Continually evaluate whether your items are still serving their purpose for you. It's critical that the volume in your home stays at a manageable level. Decluttering is a constant, lifelong pursuit. Decluttering will become as second nature as putting on shoes—the habits will become automatic. But, until you get to that point, you must consciously think about maintenance strategies.

One In, One Out

To keep the volume of items in your home manageable and to keep clutter at bay, use the one in and one out strategy. When a new item enters the home, something else needs to leave. I know it sounds tough! So, have a donation bag handy. If you bought a new coat, donate an old coat or something similar from your wardrobe. When you purchase a new kitchen gadget, look in your cupboard and find something that doesn't get used.

This handful of guidelines can help:

- Declutter young children's clothes and toys twice a year. They grow and change quickly.
- Declutter all other areas once a year.
- Make donations frequently. Don't put donations in the garage, where they can mix with other items or, worse, find their way back into the house. Put donation bags on the passenger seat of the car.

Recap – The Clutter Clearing System

Deciding how to start an organizing project can feel overwhelming, which is why we follow the Clutter Clearing System. It helps you approach each project in smaller, more manageable chunks.

Here is a recap of the main topics and strategies covered in this chapter:

Step 1: Form a Vision for the Space	Walk through your home and ask yourself the following: <ul><li>What are the activities that occur in this room?</li><li>What activities *should* occur in this room?</li><li>What items don't belong in this room?</li><li>How do you want this room to feel?</li></ul>
Step 2: Sort and Let Go	Sort items into the following categories: <ul><li>Items to keep</li><li>Items to donate (black trash bags)</li><li>Trash (white trash bags)</li><li>Recycling (tall leaf bags)</li><li>Shredding (see Resources page for link to guide)</li><li>Items belonging in another room</li><li>Items missing a part</li></ul>
Two Golden Rules	<ul><li>80 percent of a closet or cabinet is full</li><li>Make decisions only about your own items</li></ul>

Tough Decisions	• The gift you received – you get to choose what you keep • Family heirlooms – choose a small symbol • Memorabilia – stick to your space boundary • Should I sell it? – try for two weeks • I may need this item one day – can you replace it for $20 in 20 minutes? • I can reuse this item – is it taking prime storage real estate? • This cost a lot of money – it's a sunk cost; if you are out of storage, then let it go • Gift closet – stick to one shelf only
Step 3: Assign a Home	• Zoning – store similar items together • Frequency of use – how often do you need it? • Use shelving – don't stack heavy bins • Store items with your lifestyle in mind
Step 4: Contain and Label	• Measure first, buy containers later • Use clear containers for smaller items • Label clearly
Step 5: Evaluate and Maintain	• Are your storage solutions working? • Adjust organizational systems as needed • Declutter children's rooms twice a year • Declutter all other areas once a year • Make donations frequently

Notes

What ideas spoke to you?

_____
_____
_____
_____

In the Words of Our Clients

Thank you for all of your assistance helping me downsize my home and clear the way for my future. The little nagging at the back of my mind is gone.

Everything has a place and is now in its place. I just didn't know how to go about doing it. You took what was hard for me and made it easy!

I REALLY appreciate you taking away my donations. They're gone! I don't miss them, and I only have the most important-to-me things in my home now.

I now am able to find things quickly and am focusing on my future and what's important to me.

–SIMPLIFY EXPERTS CLIENT

CONCLUSION

We want to thank you for taking the journey through the six common behavior types of disorganized people and the Clutter Clearing System. Hopefully, this book has helped you identify the disorganization points in your own life and has given you a few tools and suggestions to begin solving them. Whether you think you are power shopper, a paper magnet, a caregiver, a hobbyist, easily distracted, or an overburdened employee, you deserve a life where your ability to thrive is not being held back by chronic disorganization.

This is a journey that does not end with reading this book. It is a beginning. You now have the tools to help you decide what things you really need and how you might organize them. Imagine living a decluttered life where you can easily accomplish tasks, find things quickly, and finally relax.

You can do it! Take the first step—declutter and thrive!

RESOURCES

CHADD - ADHD resource	Chadd.org
Paper shredding guidelines	Consumer.ftc.gov/blog/2015/05/pack-rats-guide-shredding
Evernote Productivity App	Evernote.com
Look up value of donated items	Goodwill.org
Focus App - music for focus	FocusAtWill.com
Institute for Challenging Disorganization (ICD)	ChallengingDisorganization.org
National Association of Productivity & Organizing Professionals (NAPO)	Napo.net
Opt-out of junk mail offers	OptOutPrescreen.com
Pomodoro Technique	Francescocirillo.com/pages/Pomodoro-Technique
Stopping Overshopping (Dr. April Lane Benson, Ph.D.)	ShopaholicNoMore.com
Unsubscribe from catalogs	CatalogChoice.org
Wunderlist – Productivity App	Wunderlist.com

THANK YOU

This book never would have been realized without our clients who reached out for help when their lives became too overwhelming. Thank you for your courage and for letting us into your lives. It's always an honor to work with you. Your stories have helped inspire others to come forward and get help.

To all our colleagues, friends, and family members who have supported this book effort through its many iterations, we couldn't have done it without you. A special thank you to Fabienne Fredrickson, Andrew Mellen, Ian Allan, Bruce Taylor, Kate Varness, Myriam Gabriel-Pollock, and Brian Hillger, who provided feedback and editing on many drafts. To Liz Fulton, Sheila Storrer and Amy Maher, thank you for letting me think out loud during our walks and for sharing your own stories and strategies. To Nicole Gebhardt and Crystal Yeagy of Niche Pressworks, thank you for your invaluable expertise and support during this process; we are indebted to you. Finally, a huge thank you to the entire Simplify Experts team: Amy Nelson, Pam Doxsie, Alicia Lott, Lovena Laycock, Paula Bordenet, Alison Grabicki, and Margie Fortman—your passion and commitment to helping our clients declutter and thrive is outstanding.

To our readers, thank you for devoting what precious time you have to learning about disorganization and how you can begin to thrive in spite of your frenetic life.

We want to hear from you! Share your disorganization stories with us. Tell us how this book has helped you. Share this book with others who struggle with disorganization. As they say, it takes a village.

With gratitude,

Denise Allan and Vlasta Hillger

Contact us:
Info@SimplifyExperts.com
SimplifyExperts.com
Facebook.com/SimplifyExperts

Next Steps

Now that you've learned about the six behavior types of disorganized people and the Clutter Clearing System, wouldn't it be nice to put all that knowledge into action?

Visit **SimplifyExperts.com**

- Download freebies and webinars
- Check out our blog and speaking events
- Book an organizing appointment

Connect with **Denise Allan** directly:

- Set up a free 20-minute get-to-know-you phone call
- Get a referral to a professional organizer in your area
- Book Denise for a speaking engagement

(425) 770-5759

Info@SimplifyExperts.com

ABOUT THE AUTHORS

Denise Allan, CPO, CPO-CD is a Certified Professional Organizer who started her business, Simplify Experts, in 2007.

It was Denise's kindergarten teacher who first saw her potential as a professional organizer. She knew long before Denise did, that helping others simplify and organize their lives would be her biggest passion. On Denise's report card, she commented that "Denise should stop organizing her table mates' art supplies and work on her own projects." Even at age six, Denise was at it organizing other people's stuff.

For many years Denise worked in the non-profit sector doing fundraising. In 2006 she craved a career change and circled back to her passion for organizing. One day it occurred to her that she had been timing her gym workouts to coincide with specific TV shows, such as TLC's reality series *Clean Sweep* and HGTV's *Mission Organization*. On these programs, professional organizers such as Peter Walsh worked with families over two days to clean out and transform their cluttered spaces. She always stayed around at the gym long enough to see the big reveal at the end of the episode. Denise was so inspired by these transformations that she took a leap of faith and started her own organizing company.

Denise is super passionate about her work. Who knew that her path to becoming a professional organizer would begin in the Duniway Elementary morning kindergarten class?

Today Denise has a team of professional organizers on staff at Simplify Experts who all share her passion for organizing and empowering others to declutter and thrive.

Denise is a member of the National Association of Productivity and Professional Organizers (NAPO). She is very active with the Institute for Challenging Disorganization (ICD) and has earned their highest accreditation of Master Trainer in Chronic Disorganization that only 23 organizers share worldwide. She has specialized training for Attention Deficit Disorder and is the past president of the ADD Resources board. She has been a frequent guest on King 5/Kong television news and has also been featured on the first three seasons of the A&E television series *Hoarders*. She is a frequent and popular speaker in the Seattle area. She volunteers her time with the Washington Women's Foundation. Reach Denise at **denise@SimplifyExperts.com**.

Vlasta Hillger is a Seattle-based writer, blogger, professional organizer, wife, and mother to two teenage sons. She believes organizing is about simplicity and practical spatial placement of the items in our homes. It wasn't until Vlasta had children that she realized just how much being organized helped her cope with the demands of motherhood. When her son was in third grade he was diagnosed with ADHD and anxiety. He had always been an energetic child who couldn't sit still long enough to eat dinner and was happiest doing any active sport. But he became anxious at school and impulsive and frustrated at home. When he began to struggle at school and received his diagnosis, Vlasta educated herself about ADHD and anxiety and used her organizational skills to create a home environment where her son could thrive. She reduced distractions in her home to help her son focus on homework and daily routines. She worked on consistently practicing daily routines, fostering self-reliance and independence in her son. She continually reduced clutter and any other visual noise, to reduce her son's anxiety. She began to understand that more than ever, maintaining a calm, organized home was critical for her son and family.

About the Authors

Vlasta credits her Czech heritage for her pragmatism and no-nonsense approach to home organizing. She finds solitude in reading and sanity in practicing yoga. Vlasta is a graduate of the University of California, Santa Barbara where she earned a bachelor's degree in political science. Reach Vlasta at **vlasta@SimplifyExperts.com.**

Made in the USA
San Bernardino, CA
13 July 2018